D0875381

DATE DUE

MAY 1 7 1993			
APR 2 5			
MAY 2 0 2003			
GAYLORD			PRINTED IN U.S.A.

Social Work Practice in a Public Welfare Setting

PRAEGER SPECIAL STUDIES IN
SOCIAL WELFARE

GENERAL EDITORS

*Neil Gilbert and
Harry Specht*

Social Work Practice in a Public Welfare Setting

An Empirical Analysis

Robert J. Teare

PRAEGER SPECIAL STUDIES • PRAEGER SCIENTIFIC

Library of Congress Cataloging in Publication Data

Teare, Robert J.
    Social work practice in a public welfare setting.

    Bibliography: p.
    Includes index.
    1. Social workers—United States. 2. Job analysis. 3. Public welfare—
United States
I. Title.
HV91.T36   361.3   81-8602
ISBN 0-03-050651-4   AACR2   .

Published in 1981 by Praeger Publishers
CBS Educational and Professional Publishing
A Division of CBS, Inc.
521 Fifth Avenue, New York, New York 10017 U.S.A.

©1981 by Praeger Publishers

123456789 145 987654321

Printed in the United States of America

.

To my parents,
Alfred and Helen,
who made it important,
and to my wife, Marge,
who made it possible

Contents

Appendixes

List of Tables

List of Figures

Foreword

The unsung heros working on the front lines of public welfare programs are frequently criticized and rarely studied. Some are trained social workers, some are career civil servants, and some are paraprofessionals who are mandated by public social policy to help the needy and at the same time prevent fraud. Who are these dedicated personnel who are rarely rewarded for their work and frequently overloaded?

This pioneering study provides us with new insights about the functions of public welfare personnel. Administrators of public welfare programs have frequently wrestled with the question of who should do what in the delivery of services to public welfare recipients. Frequently, the staffing of public welfare programs has been determined more by the funding levels than by the unique or complex problems confronting clients. The effective use of professionally trained social workers in public welfare programs has long been an important issue in the minds of knowledgeable public welfare administrators. In the mid-1960s, a national report concluded that there was a significant shortage of trained social work personnel. By the early 1970s, it became clear that the shortage could not be met and that we had failed to upgrade the thousands of untrained social service personnel working in public welfare programs. In addition, when social services were separated from the provision of assistance payments, additional questions were raised about the need for professionally trained social work personnel. Although it is clear that the social work profession has been the primary force pushing for quality social services within the public welfare field, it is still not clear how the labor should be divided in public welfare programs. The job analysis study presented here represents one of the first major efforts to analyze public welfare work in order to deal with this question. This study links public welfare job activity with worker perceptions of job satisfaction.

An examination of these phenomena is critical to an increased understanding of the dynamics of public welfare employment. It is especially important to look at social work and paraprofessional practice within the context of a public welfare agency. A comprehensive approach to job analysis should include an assessment of the work to be performed, the workers themselves, and the nature of the work organization. Most of the technology for job analysis has been developed from the perspective of industrial and organizational psychology. Consequently, any comprehensive analysis of public welfare practice must take pains to include a sociological examination of the professions and the complex organizations in which they are housed. Furthermore, social work interventions derive much of their meaning from a unique orientation to the psychology of individuals as they relate to their environment and the anthropology of family customs, traditions, and religion that affect the functioning of individuals, groups, and communities.

The organizations in which these practitioners carry out their activities are far from static. Public welfare in the United States has had a unique and colorful history. The past two decades have seen many changes in public social policy. The twenty amendments to the Social Security Act alone have had a profound effect on the administration and delivery of public welfare programs. Other legislation has been extremely influential. The 1964 Economic Opportunity Act served as a major platform for organizing welfare recipients and developing the National Welfare Rights Organization. The Model Cities Act of 1967 sought to improve the lives of poor people by promoting neighborhood -projects. The Omnibus Crime Act of 1968, which created the Law Enforcement Assistance Administration, played a significant role in easing the fears and frustrations of poor people in the ghettos of our large cities. The Community Mental Health Acts of 1963 and 1975 enabled the poor to get out and stay out of large mental hospitals. The Comprehensive Employment and Training Act (CETA) of 1972 sought to help low-income people to secure and maintain jobs. This array of legislation gave rise to a variety of programs, such as Head Start and the Neighborhood Health Centers, that were designed to enhance functioning and give the poor access to the mainstream of occupational life. This framework represents only a part of the context in which public welfare organizations have operated in recent years.

There has been an emerging accountability ethic associated with the delivery of social services. This ethic generally requires: (1) a documentation of effective and ineffective interventions, (2) an in-depth knowledge of worker activities and attitudes, (3) explicit definitions of work and the training needs of staff, (4) continuous commitment to research and demonstration, and (5) sympathetic scrutiny and constructive criticism by knowledgeable analysts, both inside and outside the social work profession.

The task analysis approach has emerged as a viable tool for analyzing public welfare jobs. Many social service jobs can be clustered into job families as a foundation for building personal systems that promote opportunities for career mobility. We have also begun to identify worker competencies related to the knowledge, skills, and abilities required for effective job performance. At the same time, we have begun to measure job satisfaction as a critical component of work performance. Throughout all these developments, we have needed a conceptual breakthrough in characterizing the relationship between social service problems, social service work, and social service personnel administration.

Robert Teare is one of the architects who have been working for the past two decades on the problem of achieving clarity in the specification and measurement of social service work. As an architect of one of the breakthroughs, Professor Teare has contributed to the clarification and specification of social service problems, as reported in the first chapter of the book. His past work has also included the specification of organizational motives for the recruitment, retention, and promotion of paraprofessional staff. He has also identified the relevant work roles performed by social service generalists. And finally, in this book he has made a major contribution to the measurement of human service work through the development of a job analysis survey instrument designed to analyze worker tasks and attitues in delivering social services. This new instrument should also prove to be a valuable tool in the development of career mobility systems based on the interrelationship of job families.

It is also important to identify the tools and perspectives used by this creative researcher. Professor Teare has acquired a working knowledge of the entire range of human service programs, from public welfare to mental health, to corrections, to rehabilitation. In addition, he brings to the subject of public welfare job analysis a rich experience in industry and teaching in the management sciences. He has a keen sensitivity to the critical way in which the client's need for services affects the nature of human service work. He recognizes the significant problems in translating humanitarian concerns into legitimate work activity. And yet he is able to maintain a strong allegiance to empiricism within a climate of significant philosophical value dilemmas and social reform rhetoric.

Professor Teare has provided us with an important first step in expanding our understanding of social service technology, as reflected in public welfare jobs and work job satisfaction. This book is a significant contribution to the field of job analysis in the human services. It provides a valuable foundation for pursuing a research agenda on social service technology.

Michael J. Austin, Ph.D.
Director, Center for Social
Welfare Research
University of Washington

Preface and
Acknowledgments

This book is about social workers and social work. More specifically, it is about people who work in a public welfare agency, the work they do, and how they feel about it. It makes no attempt to resolve the many issues surrounding contemporary social work practice; its emphasis is on description rather than prescription. The workers and jobs studied, however, are representative of many that exist throughout the country. Insofar as this is true, the findings may shed light on a number of questions and suggest directions for future investigations in welfare and social service settings.

The study described in the pages that follow began late in 1975 and lasted for almost three years. It arose out of a need for a public welfare agency to answer some basic questions about its job classification system and the utilization of its workers. Like most agencies in the mid-1970s, it was struggling with changing social welfare philosophies, rapidly proliferating programs in Medicaid and food assistance, federalization of selected public assistance programs, and the increasing role of the courts in the formulation of personnel administration policies and practices. The need to assimilate new types of workers—paraprofessionals as well as graduates of baccalaureate programs in social work—made the task of administering this agency a formidable one indeed.

The scope of work for the research effort fell broadly into four major areas. First, it was necessary to determine the correspondence or "fit" between existing job titles and descriptions in the agency's classification system and the work actually being performed by its personnel. Second, agency management believed that it needed information about worker attitudes toward job content, job attributes, conditions of work (for example, salary, promotion opportunities, supervision), and the general agency environment. This knowledge of work content and worker attitudes had to be obtained before undertaking the third task—grouping activities and jobs into a framework that could provide for "streams" of practice as well as career progressions. Finally, there was a need to arrange these practice streams into an ordered hierarchy upon which salary levels could be based. This book will describe that work in considerable detail.

Data were collected in the state public welfare agency in Alabama. It is a free-standing (nonumbrella) department of state government and is the designated Title XX agency for the state. During the period of the study, the department administered 28 service programs to its clients. In 1977, as the study was drawing to a close, the department was providing services to almost 77,000 clients. Approximately 4,000 people are employed by the agency. All are state employees and, with the exception of the commissioner, are covered by the state merit system. All jobs in the department are classified (that is, designated by a title and a capsule summary of work performed). Applicants for any job are screened and selected from a register of incumbents who have successfully completed a state civil service examination. Job classification, salary schedules, and examination procedures are supervised by a separate and autonomous state personnel board.

The programs of the agency are supervised by the state office and directly administered by the counties. There is a departmental office located in each county. In addition to direct service provision, the agency provides an increasing number of services through interagency agreements and contracts with public and private vendors. The agency supplements (with state funds) the federalized public assistance programs and directly administers Aid to Dependent Children (ADC) payments. As stated earlier, the department has a rapidly growing food assistance (food stamp) program, carries out screening for Medicaid, and has a Work Incentive (WIN) program.

The situation in the department was not unlike that of many other public welfare agencies. That is, there was a need to create a stable, sensible technology to undergird an organization that had to be responsive to changing programs and patterns of manpower utilization. Although it was typical of many public welfare departments, the agency was unique in a number of respects. Foremost among these was a commitment to the development of an empirical, research-oriented approach in addressing the issues. I was given ready access to employees at all levels of the agency. Knowledgeable people in key positions gave freely of their time; without their insight, the study would have floundered at many points. Although there was a pressing need for answers, sufficient time was allowed so that data collection instruments could be grounded in up-to-date theory and could be pretested when necessary. Relatively sophisticated data reduction techniques were used. Several times, data had to be rerun through modified programs to facilitate interpretation. Each time, the agency provided time and resources for this to be done. This progressive attitude has resulted in a set of products that have proved to be sound and useful to the agency. By the same token, it has resulted in a set of tools and procedures that may prove useful to others.

This book will describe those tools, procedures, and products. It is basically a report of a research effort that goes far beyond the typical case study. Data and data collection techniques are presented only after the theories or models that shaped them are described. This permits the reader to evaluate strengths as well as weaknesses in the approachs used and the conclusions reached. References are used sparingly in the narrative; however, all pertinent work from which the author drew has been documented. Detailed charts and tables and specimens of data collection instruments have been incorporated as appendix material.

No study of this scope can be carried out without the help of many people. This is no exception. To Harold McPheeter of the Southern Regional Educational Board, I express many thanks for a rewarding association over the past ten years. The utilization theory on which this study is based sprang from our collaborative efforts. I am deeply grateful to the sponsoring agency for its willingness to undertake this ambitious effort. To members of its top management, Gil Jennings, Burke McGonigal, and Ann Roton, goes a sincere note of thanks. Hundreds of workers contributed their time and energy in filling out questionnaires and in suggesting modifications during pretests. Without them, there would be no study. Waldo Spencer of the sponsoring agency was the agency liaison person from the beginning of the study to its end. He supervised data collection and provided invaluable knowledge of the inner workings of the personnel classification system. Judy Netzley provided editorial assistance in the early drafts of the Job Analysis Survey. Hubert Feild of Auburn University helped to cast the questionnaire into a machine-processable format. Harry and Barbara Barker of the University of Alabama contributed valuable technical assistance to the project and organized the data processing effort through use of their special program library. The actual data analysis was under the direct supervision of Don Shaver. He worked tirelessly to carry out the many computer runs, planned and unplanned.

A number of people have been instrumental in bringing the study to publication. Harry Specht recognized its potential from a limited presentation at a symposium several years ago and urged the preparation of a manuscript. I am indebted to him for his encouragement and his patience. The editorial staff at Praeger, especially Lynda Sharpe, has been most helpful. Michael Austin, who wrote the Foreword, has been a colleague for many years. He took the time to review the manuscript, and his suggestions have improved it greatly. Finally, I wish to thank Nancy Jordan. Her contributions have gone far beyond the preparation of the typescript. She formatted much of the tabular material and reacted to early versions of the copy. By managing my time as well as hers with skill and humor, she was crucial in bringing this project to completion.

Social Work
Practice in a
Public Welfare Setting

1
Manpower Utilization: Some Recent History

It was the best of times, it was the worst of times, it was the age of wisdom, it was the age of foolishness, it was the epoch of belief, it was the epoch of incredulity, it was the season of light, it was the season of darkness, it was the spring of hope, it was the winter of despair.
—*Charles Dickens, A Tale of Two Cities*

When Dickens wrote these words, he was characterizing life in France just prior to the Revolution. The next decade was to be filled with turbulence, bloodshed, violence, and sweeping change. France would never be the same. Dicken's words might well be applied to the period from 1960 to 1975 in the United States. This period, from the West Virginia primaries of the Kennedy presidential campaign to the resignation of Richard Nixon, was also filled with hope and despair. It, too, was a time of foolishness, bloodshed, and change.

INFLUENCES ON MANPOWER PLANNING

The disbelief of the period settled on many things, including most functions of government and industry. Social welfare services were no exception.[1] Challenges to social welfare programs focused most often on their relevance and effectiveness. Although no single factor can explain the widespread skepticism about social services that existed at the time, there is no doubt about its pervasive influence on social policy—including manpower planning. The manpower utilization model that is the central focus of this book grew out of that zeitgeist. For that reason, a brief overview of some of the major forces that shaped the model should provide a useful context for its presentation.

Technological Change

In the decade following World War II, a major shift took place in the economy of the United States. No longer did the production of goods predominate—we had become a service-producing society (Levine 1968; Yarmolinsky 1968). The shift was propelled by rapid technological changes in industries responding to the necessities of war. The transition was neither smooth nor orderly. In fact, workers in vulnerable production jobs were usually displaced faster than jobs in the service sector could be created to absorb them. Furthermore, transitional training programs were developed far too slowly. The result of this rapid displacement was a severe discontinuity between the skills possessed by the displaced labor force and those required by the new kinds of jobs.

The problem of technologically induced unemployment had reached major proportions by the 1960 presidential elections. The country had experienced one recession (1957–58) and would soon feel another (1960–61). The urgent nature of chronic unemployment and the emergence of poverty as a national issue were highlighted during the 1960 West Virginia presidential primaries. The blight of Appalachia offered proof that an entire region of the country could be deeply affected by the technological and economic forces at work in the country.

Changing Concepts of Poverty

In 1957, the launching of Sputnik shook the national confidence. In subsequent years, two recessions and a nagging awareness of deeply rooted social problems eroded it even further. By the early 1960s, there was widespread skepticism about the effectiveness of traditional remedies for dealing with social problems.

In 1962, Michael Harrington's *The Other America* was published. It was an indignant work. In it, Harrington argued persuasively that the country was faced with a poverty problem of a new sort. The "other America" to which he referred was populated by millions of people who lived just out of sight of the highway and who were one recession, one layoff, or one catastrophic illness away from unemployment, poverty, and welfare. The poverty Harrington talked about did not consist of isolated individuals singled out because of special disability (case poverty). Nor was it restricted to living in specific geographic areas such as West Virginia, where existing economic structures had broken down (insular poverty). He spoke rather of forces in the economy that systematically brought about the loss of a person's occupational viability. He was describing, of course, the technological changes referred to earlier in this chapter. Harrington, however, injected life into these cold, impersonal forces. He dramatized, through many illustrations, how changes in the nature of work and the division of labor had placed large numbers of people in a position of persistent economic vulnerability. Most often, these people were the very young and the elderly, ethnic minorities, and the poorly educated and the marginally trained. By linking occupational vulnerability to social class (class unemployment), Harrington helped to identify the kinds of people and problems that would need to be addressed in developing an "active" manpower policy designed to remedy the situation.

Harrington dwelt on the persistence of poverty and the inherent determinism in the economic forces that were operative at the time. The issue of chronic poverty had been raised several years earlier by Galbraith (1958), but Harrington talked at length about its pervasiveness and about the feelings of helplessness, frustration, and alienation that resulted from the continual struggle to reach the mainstream of the job market.

Harrington's work had both political and theoretical impact. It is credited with crystallizing John Kennedy's determination to develop a poverty program in 1963 (Schlesinger 1965). This created the momentum that eventually led to the legislative program now known as the War on Poverty. The psychic demoralization so graphically described by Harrington prompted other theorists to write about the cultural aspects of poverty (Bergel 1962; Roach and Gursalin 1967). Prolonged coping with disadvantage and poverty was believed to produce attitudes unique to the poor, which would separate them from those who would provide help. The presumed barrier of this psychological distance would later become dogma in the drive to use indigenous workers to provide services to the poor (Reiff and Riessman 1964).

New Legislative Programs

This altered thinking produced changing legislative responses. In May 1961, the Area Redevelopment Act (ARA) was passed. It sprang from the Kennedy experience in Appalachia and was designed to provide massive economic assistance to defined geographic areas. The programs it authorized were predicated on the assumption that economic rehabilitation could not take place unless manpower was recognized as a resource to be developed and protected. For the first time, a federal program reflected the human resource utilization philosphy, which can be found in the manpower field to this day.

In 1962, the Manpower Development and Training Act (MDTA) authorized training and retaining programs of up to one year for unemployed youth (aged 17 years or older). Also eligible were workers who were facing displacement due to technological change. This was the first manpower program to extend coverage to the vulnerable worker.

In 1964, the poverty program envisioned by Kennedy came into being with the passage of the Economic Opportunity Act (EOA). It differed from its predecessors in that it emphasized the participation of residents of the communities to be served. Recipients were expected to be involved in the planning and delivery of services. It is obvious that the spirit behind this legislation closely resembled the philosophy of Riessman and his associates (Pearl 1965). Over the next several years, an outpouring of legislation radically altered manpower planning in the service sector of the economy.[2] By 1970, the labor force in human services (welfare, health, education, mental health, vocational rehabilitation, and law enforcement) was being energized—some would say paralyzed—by 100 separate grant-in-aid programs authorized under 35 different acts of Congress and administered by 8 departments and agencies (Teare 1978).

CONFLICTING MANPOWER UTILIZATION MOTIVES

The result of this outpouring of interest and resources was a great deal of motion but little direction. Suddenly it seemed as if everyone—the government, client groups, the professions—was interested in manpower utilization. An immense and fragmented literature, focusing mainly on the use of paraprofessional workers, came into being (U.S. Department of Health, Education and Welfare 1974). It dealt with training, job design, worker assimilation, career mobility, recruitment, selection, deployment, placement, and an assortment of other manpower functions and issues. This material seemed to be without any organizing principle, however. It was a technopolitical potpourri of much rhetoric and little science. A few writers have tried to make sense of the driving forces underlying this burgeoning movement (Grosser 1969; Katan 1974; Gatewood and Teare 1976). Their analyses of the disparate objectives and the inconsistencies inherent within them are worth a brief review.

Solving the Manpower Shortage

In 1965, the manpower gap in social welfare was discovered. In that year, an influential government report (U.S. Department of Health, Education and Welfare 1965) jolted a number of professions by pointing to a widening disparity between the social service needs of people throughout the country and the manpower available to meet those needs. The report established the fact, long suspected, that large numbers of workers without full educational preparation were employed in service agencies throughout the country. This widespread practice of "underfilling" was ascribed to a nationwide shortage of fully trained professionals. The dire predictions of shortage contained in the report were based on the assumption that federal and state funding for human service programs would continue to increase through the end of the decade and into the 1970s. This did not happen, of course; and the gap failed to widen to any appreciable degree. Despite this, the impression that a crucial shortage of service workers existed would persist as a dominant theme in the manpower literature for some time. It would not be the only theme.

Providing Employment for the Poor

With a manpower shortage in the service sector and chronic unemployment in the production sector, it was inevitable that the delivery system for social services would be selected as a vehicle for providing jobs for the poor and the unemployed. This indeed took place. With the passage of the Harris Amendments to the Social Security Act in 1967, publicly funded social service programs were mandated to provide training and employment opportunities for former recipients. This effort, which was minimal, focused on the provision of entry-level employment. It was soon recognized that this was not enough. Entry-level really meant "dead-end." The "new careers" philosophy espoused by Riessman and his colleagues argued for continued employment, vocational support services, and upward mobility through career opportunity (Reiff and Riessman 1964). As support for this philosophy grew, a relatively simple goal was transformed into a complex one.

Providing Therapeutic Work Experiences

The rationale behind the objective of providing therapeutic work experience comes from the "helper therapy" principle described by

Riessman (1965). The principle has two central theses: (1) that the use of individuals with problems (usually drug abuse, mental illness, or alcoholism) in helping roles will produce benefits for the helpers, and (2) that, as these improvements occur, the helpers will become more effective workers and will have a positive impact on the clients. The strategy had some appeal, but it was difficult to implement. Large social service systems did not have time for the careful placements and close supervision that such a mechanism required. Furthermore, the social services seemed to lack clearly analogous situations in which such a principle would be operative. Finally, there was little hard evidence to support the principle. All these factors, coupled with the risks inherent in such an employment strategy, caused it to fade quickly into the background as a major manpower utilization motive.

Increasing Service Effectiveness

As mentioned earlier, continual coping with poverty was presumed to produce an attitude pattern that was unique to the poor and the disadvantaged. This theoretical proposition gradually gained credence and became the basis for assertions about the irrelevance and ineffectiveness of social services. The assertions were made in a variety of ways. Some writers contended that prolonged education socialized service workers in ways that impeded understanding of client needs. Others stressed social class and ethnic barriers between helpers and clients. Whatever the variation, the theme was the same—service systems had drifted away from client concerns and were seen as having little impact on basic social problems. Because clients were presumed to have a unique perspective, it was believed that they could make positive contributions to the realignment of social goals and priorities. This thinking was central in the drive for increased client participation, as reflected in the language of the Economic Opportunity Act of 1964.

Increasing Service Efficiency

By the late 1960s, the service sector was feeling the presence of many new kinds of workers. Most of these workers were untrained; many had never worked before; and some were dedicated to changing the system or bringing it to a halt. How should all these different people be used? What should be the role of the workers with traditional preparation? The division of labor had become a truly knotty problem. In the service sector, especially in human services, work assignment had long been based on academic credentials. Now large numbers of people were employed without credentials and in an atmosphere of disbelief about their value. Furthermore, accusations of irrelevance and ineffectiveness had begun to cast doubt on traditional methods of intervention. These were fueled by concerns about bureaucratic waste and professional "turf" disputes. Obviously, the social services needed some rationale by which to take advantage of the unique talents and skills possessed by the many different types of workers now in service. To be most useful, such a framework had to distinguish the tasks that could be carried out by people with little or no training from those that required fully trained professionals. Only when this was done could waste be reduced and the most efficient use of diverse talents be realized.

WANTED: A MANPOWER UTILIZATION FRAMEWORK

Sources of Confusion

This was the situation in social service manpower planning by the end of the 1960s. In retrospect, it is easy to see why disorder existed. The motives just described called for widely different and often incompatible implementation methods. Solving the manpower shortage and dealing with unemployment required rapid responses. Emphasis had to be placed on recruitement techniques that would result in quick placements; it did not much matter what the workers did so long as they were working. Thus, selection and training were of secondary importance. These motives appealed most to the professions and to the public, who were interested in task relief and tax relief, respectively.[3]

Providing therapeutic work experiences involved a calculated risk and thus required a careful match between the problems of the worker and the needs of the client. Furthermore, it called for an orchestration of responsibility that implied close supervision and a knowledge of the tasks to be performed. This was also true of the service efficiency goal, which was predicated on a highly specific plan for allocating work based on skills and experience. These two motives, though similar in implementation requirements, appealed to opposing constituencies. The new workers liked the therapeutic benefits (and the money) associated with working, while the reduction of waste and inefficiency had great appeal to the agencies and the professions.

Increasing the effectiveness of service became a rallying point for clients, which made it threatening to the professions. Agencies were further intimidated by this motive because it had been legitimized by Congress. Clients now had a vehicle (through the Economic Opportunity Act) by which they might become a part of the delivery system itself. Effective participation, however, presumed that clients' roles would be clearly defined and that the inevitable disputes arising between workers and client-participants would be resolved. Neither of these conditions occurred very often.

By now it should be obvious that dealing with manpower issues in the social services during this period had become a truly perplexing process. Since various pressure groups argued for opposing objectives, priorities were hard to establish. Once established, they were difficult to implement because of fragmented and poorly developed technologies. Through all this confusion, at least one thing was clear—the service field needed a manpower utilization framework that could capitalize on the broad array of talents, skills, and points of view possessed by its workers.

Some Previous Attempts

The preceeding comments are not meant to imply that there were no rationales for the utilization of service workers. This was far from the case. As early as 1961, Willard Richan had proposed a scheme for assigning work based on "client vulnerability." According to Richan, clients susceptible to harm by workers who did not have "built-in social work values, knowledge, and skills" should be assigned only to fully trained professionals. However, clients who would not be damaged by this method of assignment could be served by workers with little training or skill. Three years later, Finestone (1964) suggested several strategies, among them the case unit and the task unit of differentiation. In the first strategy, cases (or clients) with severe problems would be assigned to fully trained workers, while those with less severe problems would be given to workers with less training. In the task unit of differentiation, professionals would be given the more difficult tasks, while less difficult ones would be assigned to workers with fewer years of preparation. Another plan, set forth by Anderson and Dockhorn in 1965, specified several criteria for identifying tasks that were appropriate to assign to unskilled or paraprofessional workers. The criteria involved such things as learning time and repetitiveness. Finally, in 1968, Barker and Briggs proposed that the "episode of service" be used as the basis for work assignment. By organizing agency staff into teams and focusing on such episodes, they contended that work could be effectively partitioned among workers with different levels of skill and training.[4]

Thus, between 1962 and 1968 a number of utilization plans had been put forward. These approaches had some basic similarities. First, the interventions they described usually involved casework. The plans seemed to presume that workers would be dealing primarily with deficits in clients. As a result, little attention was given to whether the plans would be applicable to work with groups or to community organization strategies. Second, all the approaches were rationales for the division of *existing* labors and, as such, made little or no provision for ways in which new service roles or functions would be developed and assigned. Finally, the schemes were all rather vague about skill differences in workers; they seemed to assume that these would arise, in the main, from differing amounts of formal education. For these and other reasons, the rationales described were not satisfactory. By 1968, the need was not for just another free-floating manpower utilization strategy but for a fundamentally different way of conceptualizing social problems and how they would be dealt with by social service delivery systems.

THE UNDERGRADUATE SOCIAL WELFARE MANPOWER PROJECT

Addressing the bill of particulars just described was a tall order. It required the development of an approach that could deal with both the purpose of labor and its division and, while so doing, could formulate a wide range of new jobs. This section describes an approach to this problem that was developed by the Southern Regional Education Board (SREB) in Atlanta.

Early in 1968, SREB received a contract from the Georgia Department of Family and Childrens' Services. This contract, made possible by a grant from the Social and Rehabilitation Service of the U. S. Department of Health, Education and Welfare, was oriented toward some of the manpower issues described earlier in this chapter. The project was a reflection of the fact that, at the time, approximately 75 percent of the social welfare positions in agencies were occupied by people with various types of baccalaureate degrees. In most instances, these people were being used in lieu of fully trained personnel (that is, those with MSW degrees), with no modification in job content to compensate for level or type of training. Given this situation, the SREB project staff was committed to the development of more rational guidelines for the use of workers with BSW and BA degrees. While concentrating on the baccalaureate worker, the staff was also concerned about formulating a framework that would have implications for a wide range of workers—from those with a few weeks of in-service training to those with the traditional professional degree.

In essence, the SREB manpower project was a job construction effort. As Fine (1967) pointed out, there are really only two ways in which this can be done. One method, called "job factoring," is basically a process of dissection. In carrying it out, existing jobs are broken down (factored) into tasks, and those tasks that are similar in content or level of difficulty are clustered together. These homogeneous task clusters become the building blocks of the "new" jobs. In many respects this method is similar to the work-simplification principles set forth by Taylor in 1911. The second method, called the "developmental method," begins with an analysis of needs and goals. After goals are defined, a systematic deductive process is used to develop tactics for meeting those goals. The tactics are then redefined in terms of tasks and activities that can be grouped into jobs in a variety of ways.

It is obvious that the two methods are very different.[5] Job factoring should be used only when one can assume that the work currently being done is relevant and appropriate, because the basic pool of tasks remains unchanged; only the task groupings are altered. If the assumption of relevance is questionable, the developmental method should be used. It permits goals to be redefined. If new goals emerge, entirely new tasks may be identified; and if old needs no longer exist, existing tasks may be dropped.

The SREB Project Approach

Because of the prevailing climate of skepticism, the SREB project staff opted in favor of the developmental method. In other words, the staff believed that service goals needed to be examined. With this process in mind, a series of symposia was planned for the fall of 1968. Four two-day sessions were held at three-to four-week intervals at a resort near Atlanta. Each symposium was designed to implement a separate phase of the developmental method. There were approximately 13 participants at each session, all carefully selected so that a balance among points of view would be likely. Most participants were social workers, but the fields of corrections, education, rehabilitation, law, and public personnel were also represented. Several participants were representing advocacy groups. Some participants, a "core faculty," attended all four sessions in order to provide continuity.

In the first session, the participants were asked to identify the needs and problems of the public that they believed to be within the purview of the social welfare service system. They were to emphasize those needs that were not currently being met. Once the needs were identified, they would be grouped into a descriptive framework.

In the second session, the problems and needs identified in the previous session were used to infer the goals and purposes of contemporary social services. The participants were then asked to develop activities and tasks that would be likely to meet these goals. It was understood that these activities might be tentative and more like strategies for intervention than job definitions. No attempt was made to assign tasks to specific types of workers or to disciplines.

The third session concentrated on the realities of service delivery. Participants were asked to identify the constraints placed on social welfare because of the needs of the professions and the workers in they system. This session focussed on the impacts of the "establishment" (professions, funding sources) on the organization and management of work activity in the social services.

In the fourth session, the participants concentrated on work activities. They were to add tasks that arose from the needs of service staffs to those that had been inferred (in the second session) from the needs of clients and the public. They were also asked to develop a rationale for clustering the various tasks into meaningful job configurations.

The SREB Model

The symposium series achieved most of its objectives. In the first session, approximately 90 illustrations of specific problems and needs were generated. Participants had more difficulty identifying tasks, but the second session did result in a good beginning in this area. The symposium participants were especially articulate in identifying constraints on the delivery system (third session). Their combined frustrations generated many suggestions for change. The final session, however, did not produce a well-organized rationale for grouping tasks and activities. Thus, although they yield from the four sessions was rich in detail and diversity, the material still lacked organization.

In the months following the symposia, the SREB project staff conducted numerous workshops throughout the Southeast. In each, symposium findings were discussed, issues were outlined, and reactions were sought. This process of repeated presentation served to crystallize the material, and an overall conceptualization was finally developed.[6] Its essential feature is the representation of social welfare problems in terms of a three-dimensional grid (see Figure 1.1). The three interacting dimensions of the cube reflect the proposition that, when service workers deal with social problems, they attempt to maintain or alter the status of functioning of target groups (that is, clients, groups, organizations, or communities) in one or more domains of living by dealing with or overcoming various obstacles to functioning. Before proceeding further, some discussion of each of the dimensions contained in this framework is in order.

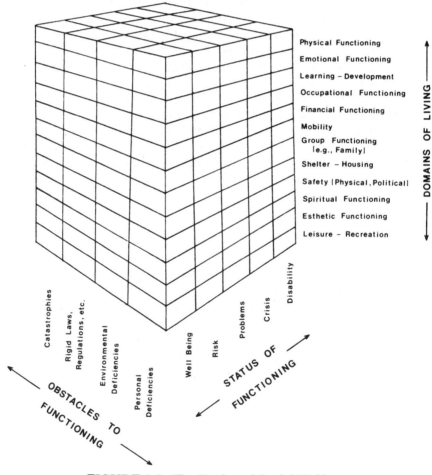

FIGURE 1.1. The Realm of Social Welfare

Domains of Living

As stated earlier, the symposia participants identified hundreds of problems in their attempts to deal with the range of client, family, and community needs that they perceived to be the purview of social welfare. These problems touched on many different areas of living. A more convenient characterization had to be found, and so the needs and problems were grouped into subject matter categories according to the manifest content reflected by them. These subject areas were called *domains of living*. They represent the different spheres of human existence in which individuals, groups, and social institutions attempt to function. These twelve domains are not seen as mutually exclusive or exhaustive. The divisions are rather arbitrary and could be partitioned into a greater or lesser number of categories. Often, when the symposia participants described real problem situations, they indicated that they were called upon to deal simultaneously with problems in more than one domain (the classic multiproblem client). The conceptualization of multiple domains permits target groups to be characterized in this manner.

Obstacles to Functioning

If there were no difficulties in meeting basic needs, social services would not be necessary. This obviously is not the case; numerous forces block individuals, families, or groups from meeting needs and functioning at optimum levels. The participants dwelt at length on these forces. Generally, they talked about obstacles that were classifiable into four major categories:

1. Personal deficiencies: inadequacies internal to individuals, such as lack of education or training, poor health, personal instability, or inappropriate values.
2. Environmental deficiencies: lack of resources or access to them within the setting in which the target group is operating, for example, lack of housing, shortage of jobs, absence of public transportation, lack of adequate medical facilities.
3. Rigid or inequitable laws and regulations: legislation, policies, or practices that impose unfair restrictions, such as punitive eligibility requirements, inconsistent governmental regulations, discrimination in employment, "redlining" of neighborhoods by lending institutions.
4. Catastrophes: unplanned or unanticipated events that have tragic consequences, such as the death of a breadwinner, a disabling illness, or the destruction of a home by fire or flood.

The combination of obstacles and domains is almost limitless and gives evidence of the fact that social welfare workers are confronted with an endless array of these situations as they attempt to intervene on behalf of their clients.

Status of Functioning

As the participants described their activities, they often reflected their frustration at being unable to do little more than "pick up the pieces" after a crisis had occurred in the life of a client or family. They wanted to be involved earlier in the development of the problem. Just as often, they talked about the disastrous effects of an illness or a death, which resulted in the rapid precipitation of a crisis. A common thread running through many of their descriptions was the notion of a *continuum* of functioning. A social problem occurs when there is a movement, gradual or swift, of the client system along this continuum in one or more domains of living. Very often, a deterioration of functioning in one domain (for example, physical) triggers movement in others (for example, occupational, financial, shelter, emotional). These predictable dominolike scenarios are the natural histories that social welfare workers try to interrupt through their interventions. In the model, this continuum has been made explicit, and five levels have been identified.

1. Well-being: At this level of functioning, all indicators would suggest the absence of any problems.
2. Risk: In this situation, although no manifest signs may exist, the target group is clearly in jeopardy by virtue of the natural history of problem development. (This is the level of functioning so poignantly illustrated by Harrington in *The Other America*.)
3. Problems: At this level, difficulties are in evidence, but they can still be handled with the resources of the target group.
4. Crisis: At this point, available coping mechanisms are no longer able to deal with stresses and problems, so outside support or intervention has become necessary. Theoretically, restoration to well-being is still possible, but it is difficult at this stage. (Time and again the participants lamented the fact that scarce resources and restrictive eligibility policies forced them to wait until the crisis stage before they could provide services.)
5. Disability: When this level is reached, the client system has been permanently altered by the difficulties encountered. Most often, return to well-being is not possible, and certain problems can be expected to be of a chronic or continuous nature.

Goals and Objectives of Social Welfare

The concepts of a continuum of functioning and a natural history are really the cornerstones of the framework. Without the belief that many social welfare problems progress through a predictable sequence of chronological stages (the natural history), the setting of differential goals for intervention would be impossible. Throughout the symposia, the participants speculated on the major points of intervention in social problems. From these discussions, four basic social welfare goals were identified:

1. Promotion of positive social functioning: activities that are directed toward client systems functioning at a level of well-being. These interventions are designed to enhance self- or community-actualization. Problem prevention is a by-product of these activities.
2. Prevention: intervention that takes place at the risk stage of problem development. It is aimed at removing obstacles or barriers to need-fulfillment.
3. Treatment: activities that occur at the problem or crisis stage in which the primary objective is the elimination of the acute difficulties being experienced by the client system. The participants identified this, with some rancor, as the traditional role of the social service worker.
4. Maintenance: activities that are directed toward client systems no longer able to cope with problems. These interventions are usually continuous activities and are often required for long periods of time.

Throughout the symposium series, emphasis was placed on the need to identify the tasks and activities implied by the goals just described. The participants were not always able to do this, not as a result of shortcomings on their part but rather because, in social welfare, there is often no one best way to achieve a stated goal. For any given problem, a number of approaches might be taken to deal with it. Furthermore, a specific activity might result in a range of consequences.

Thus, the symposium groups were not able to prescribe exact pathways for achieving goals and meeting needs. They spoke instead about a greater number of intermediate objectives, which they felt should become the underlying themes for optional strategies of intervention. Nine objectives were synthesized from the variety of approaches suggested by the participants:

1. Detection: identification of individuals, groups, or structures that are experiencing crisis or are vulnerable (at risk) and identification of conditions in the environment that are causing problems or increasing risks.
2. Linkage: physical connection of a client system with existing sources of help or connection of elements of the service delivery system with one another.

3. Advocacy: active removal of obstacles or barriers that prevent people from exercising rights, receiving benefits, or using needed resources.
4. Mobilization: the assembling and energizing of new or existing groups, resources, organizations, or structures to deal with problems or to prevent them from occurring.
5. Instruction: conveying information and knowledge, increasing awareness, and developing skills in others.
6. Behavior change: bringing about modification in behavior, attitudes, values, and perceptions of various client systems.
7. Information processing: collection, classification, and analysis of data (about clients, organizations, communities) within a social welfare context.
8. Administration: planning, direction, control, and evaluation of a facility, organization, program, or service unit.
9. Continuing care: provision of ongoing treatment and support on an extended basis. These activities can be carried out in institutional, community, or home settings.

These nine intermediate objectives were seen by the SREB staff as the centers of gravity of social welfare. Each was viewed as an option to be selected only if it suited the needs of the situation. The model therefore permits one to conceive of social welfare practice as a blend of these options. The more limited the blend, the more specialized the practice. It should be emphasized that these nine objectives are *not* methods; they are ends rather than means. In job analysis parlance, they are "what gets done" not "what people do."

CONCLUDING COMMENTS

As stated earlier, the symposium did not get very far in identifying a great number of specific tasks and activities. Nevertheless, the framework that resulted represented a considerable departure from previous thinking. As a practice model, it took, a broader view than most of its predecessors. It implied that no single method or technique was adequate for dealing with contemporary social problems. It encouraged manpower planners to proceed simultaneously along innovative and traditional lines. It emphasized maintenance as much as prevention, change as much as stability, care as much as cure. Its most striking feature was its depiction of social welfare practice as a blend of activities and tasks, flowing out of objectives, with the mixture of tasks varying as the situation requires. Since the task is the central building block, job composition could be altered by changing the level and type of tasks included in the job.

Much work remained to be done, however, in the area of task definition and analysis. The SREB project was the catalyst for several subsequent activites, which are described in the next chapter. As they are presented, their influence on the methodology used in this book will become obvious.

NOTES

1. The term *social welfare services* can be defined in different ways. As used here, it corresponds to the broad array of services, both public and private, that are designed to support individual and community functioning and to alleviate social problems. For more elaboration of this general concept see, among others, Gilbert and Specht 1974, and Teare and McPheeters 1970.

2. Other legislation included the Scheuer Amendments to EOA (1966); the Allied Health Professionals Training Act (1966); Amendments to the Higher Education Act (1967); Amendments to the Elementary and Secondary Education Act (1967); the Harris Amendments to the Social Security Act (1967); Amendments to the Vocational Rehabilitation Act (1968); Amendments to the Vocational Education Act (1968); the Omnibus Crime Control and Safe Streets Act (1968); Amendments to the Juvenile Delinquency and Control Act (1968); the Health Manpower Act (1968); and Amendments to the EOA (1969).

3. For an analysis of the beneficiaries of various manpower utilization motives, see Katan (1974).

4. For more detailed descriptions of these approaches, including an evaluation of their strengths and weaknesses, see the excellent summaries by Barker and Briggs (1966, 1968).

5. A more detailed analysis of these two job construction methods can be found in Teare (1978), pp. 75–80.

6. A detailed account of the symposium and the evolution of the model can be found in Teare and McPheeters (1970).

The Evolution of a
Task Analysis Approach

SOME EARLY EFFORTS

The National Study of Social Welfare and
Rehabilitation Workers

In 1968, the Social and Rehabilitation Service (SRS) of the U.S. Department of Health, Education and Welfare (HEW) began an ambitous study of workers in social welfare and rehabilitation.[1] The study was designed by SRS staff, and it relied heavily on research procured through contracts and grants to individuals in academic and research organizations. (I was principal investigator for one of the SRS-funded contracts associated with this national study.) The SRS project is important to the study described in this book for several reasons. First, it was stimulated by the HEW report mentioned in the previous chapter and reflected the growing importance then being placed by the federal government on manpower problems in the service sector (U.S. Department of Health, Education and Welfare 1965). Consequently, it helped to focus attention on issues in the utilization of social service and rehabilitation workers. At a more personal level, it gave me an opportunity to compile and evaluate the literature on the content of work performed by social service workers and to assess the status of task analysis methodology.

The component of the national study undertaken by my staff and I focused on an investigation of the employment practices (selection, utilization, evaluation) of paraprofessional workers in social services and rehabilitation. Our project, which lasted from 1971 to 1973, was charged with the development and field-testing of selected data collection instruments and methodology, which would later be incorporated into the national study. One of the instruments resulting from this effort is a distant ancestor of the questionnaire that is central to this book.

In its early stage, the SRS questionnaire was necessarily brief, since it was but one of many instruments in the then-unfolding national study. Basically, it was a task analysis schedule consisting of task fragments that had been grouped arbitrarily into 26 clusters. Clustering was done solely on a logical basis (content), around roles and objectives generated from the SREB symposia. Respondents were asked to estimate the number of hours they spent each week in carrying out the activities described in each of the clusters. For each task on which at least one hour was spent, the respondents answered questions using a series of Likert scales. They described the amount of discretion permitted in the task, its benefit to the client, its importance and difficulty, and the satisfaction derived from doing it.

Pilot work for the national study was carried out in 1972. Although the pilot was limited (it involved fewer than 100 workers), it helped to provide some answers that would prove useful in later work. First, the pilot demonstrated that the roles suggested by the participants in the SREB symposia did, in fact, exist. Distinct patterns of work, consistent with several of the SREB roles, emerged from the analysis of findings. Second, it seemed feasible to use a self-report task analysis format for describing a wide range of jobs. If the task content was sufficiently comprehensive, job differences could be reflected through the use of subgrouping techniques. Finally, the pilot work demonstrated the need to include supplementary information, such as demographic data, along with the task data in order to explain patterns in job activity.

The Florida Board of Regents Study

In 1972, the usefulness of the embryonic job survey (later to be called the Job Analysis Survey, or JAS) was limited, because its content was confined largely to work performed by paraprofessionals and workers trained at the baccalaureate level. To be more useful, task statements appropriate to other levels of workers would have to be added. In this same year, the Board of Regents of the State University System of Florida began a project that would help with this type of problem in the instrument.

The Florida project, also funded by the Social and Rehabilitation Service of HEW, lasted from 1972 to 1975. It established an Office of Career Planning and Curriculum Development for the Human Services (OCP) within the Board of Regents in Tallahassee. This office was to be the manpower-planning liaison between the university system and the Florida Department of Health and Rehabilitative Services (HRS), which was the human services "umbrella" agency for the state.

HRS was a large agency. With more than 15,000 employees, it had a host of personnel and manpower problems. It was essentially a loose confederation of previously independent agencies, and it had a fragmented personnel classification system. There were few classifications for the jobs held by the 10,000 employees at the lower levels and many classifications for the jobs at the top. Workers doing similar work in different divisions were paid different salaries. In most of the divisions, no clear rationale existed for either lateral or vertical job mobility. In short, the department was a good example of the disarray that passed for manpower utilization at that time.

Basic Project Approach

There was an obvious need for a solid base of information about the job activities of HRS employees. Accordingly, the OCP staff embarked on an ambitious program of technical assistance and organizational change.[2] At the heart of this effort was the construction of a bank of task data that would describe the work activities of all unlicensed employees in the agency. To do this, a carefully stratified sample of 747 people was drawn from the population of slightly more than 14,500 employees. First, these people were given a 34-item biographical questionnaire to gather data about work and worker characteristics. Then a work diary, essentially a five-day work sample, was used to compile information about work performed. Respondents used a standard format to describe each task, to indicate its duration, and to specify its frequency.

In this manner, an initial pool of 30,000 specific task statements was generated. These statements were screened by experienced workers. Statements that described the same task, despite differences in setting and client, were grouped together. These tasks were further refined and synthesized into 358 representative task descriptions (RTDs). The RTDs became the cornerstone of a proposed manpower information system for the agency.

Characteristics of the Tasks

The 358 tasks, which came to be called the Florida Task Bank, still had to be organized in some way. The OCP staff decided to use the SREB roles, described in Chapter 1, as the organizing framework.

Panels of experts took each RTD and assigned it to one of the 11 roles outline in the Teare and McPheeters (1970) monograph. Within each role, a number of more specific subcategories or substantive areas were identified. These 11 roles and 21 substantive areas are depicted in Table 2.1. As part of the development of the RTDs, a number of salient task characteristics were identified and measured. Each task was rated, using several functional job analysis (FJA) scales, according to procedures described by Fine and Wiley (1971). These scales dealt with the orientation of the task (relative involvement with things, data, and people), implied prescription and discretion, and educational development required for performance. The OCP staff also developed scales by which the difficulty and the consequence of error of each task was evaluated.

When completed, the Florida Task Bank consisted of 358 carefully

TABLE 2.1
Content Areas of the Florida Task Bank

Role	Substantive Area	Number of Tasks
Broker	Arranging services	13
Consumer Advocate	Advocating for individuals	2
Activator	Developing resources and support	6
Systems Advocate	Generating support for change	1
Counselor	Guiding/advising consumers	17
	Coaching/training consumers	26
Consultant	Training staff/laypersons	15
	Exchanging knowledge with colleagues	4
Rehabilitator	Providing behavior treatment	10
Care Giver	Regulating activities	12
	Providing physical/medical assistance	10
	Providing daily living care	33
Client Programmer	Collecting/recording consumer information	23
	Planning/organizing services	15
	Evaluating/processing consumer information	14
Systems Researcher	Collecting/organizing/reporting operational information	15
Administrator	Coordinating	27
	Planning	11
	Managing personnel	33
	Monitoring procedures	27
	Carrying out support activities	44

Note: Material has been paraphrased and abbreviated to facilitate presentation.

derived human services activities couched in a standarized language. Although it built on the SREB material, it far surpassed the original in both scope and specificity. By the completion of the OCP project in 1975, an excellent foundation for task analysis had been laid down. The SREB project had developed the conceptual model; the Florida project had added breadth and detail. The time was right for a detailed application in an agency setting.

THE DEPARTMENT OF PENSIONS AND SECURITY STUDY

Issues and Problems

The opportunity to apply the SREB and Florida research came very quickly. The setting was in Alabama, in the Department of Pensions and Security (DPS)—the free-standing public welfare agency serving that state. That department was coping with a number of the same problems as HRS had in Florida. Since the early 1970s, the DPS's programs had grown rapidly, especially the food stamp and medical assistance programs. The department had also placed increasing emphasis on services delivered through vendors and contractors. These and many other changes propelled by federal participation in financing had altered the functions carried out by many of the workers in the department. This made it increasingly vulnerable to pressures to produce a more defensible rationale for job classification and worker utilization procedures.

The greatest concern was with jobs in the social worker series, a sequence of positions including most of the program-oriented personnel in the department. (By early 1976, almost 2,700 workers were employed in these positions. The series did not include maintenance, clerical, secretarial, accounting, or statistical workers. A summary of the major classifications in this series can be found in Appendix A.) The most crucial problem had to do with the correspondence between the content implied by job descriptions and the work actually being done by workers in the jobs so described. If there was a poor fit between what the workers did and what they were supposed to be doing, three major organizational problems were created. First, testing procedures based on job descriptions would no longer be valid, since they would not meet the criterion of job-relatedness. (Almost all positions in the social worker series were subject to merit-system testing procedures. Organizations using such tests must be able to document a correspondence between the content of the examination and that of the job activities, which establishes the job-relatedness of the tests.) Such a situations would place the agency in jeopardy in the event of litigation associated with selection procedures. Second, university-based as well as in-service training programs would be ineffective. Because they were designed to prepare people for specific jobs, major shifts in job content could render such programs irrelevant. Since the agency subsidized a number of training programs, a considerable sum of money was at risk. Finally, career ladders might become inappropriate, since the actual job sequences would no longer constitute an orderly progression of tasks and activities. Furthermore, gaps might exist that could only be filled by creating new positions.

In addition to these specific personnel matters, the agency had other needs. There was little information about the characteristics (for example, pace, variety, discretion level) of the tasks carried out by its service workers. No one knew very much about how employees felt about their jobs and the conditions under which they worked; it had been a long time since an attitude survey had been conducted. Consequently, if decisions were to be made about restructuring jobs and career ladders, few guidelines existed on which to base them. This was the situation in January 1975. It was obvious that an extensive effort to collect systematic job information had to be initiated.

Development of the Job Analysis Instrument

Because I had worked as a management consultant to the department, I was familiar with the personnel situation and with the significant aspects of departmental operations. As a result, in early 1975, I was placed under contract to design a job analysis procedure, to supervise the collection of data involving its use, to carry out data analyses, and to prepare appropriate recommendations.

Drawing from the work cited earlier, including the SREB material, preliminary content for the data collection was specified. Meetings were held with top administrative personnel and with people from the State Personnel Board and the Bureau of Administrative Services. (The Alabama State Personnel Board is an autonomous department of state government, created by statute, which administers the state merit system. The board is assisted in this task by a personnel bureau within each state agency—in DPS, the Bureau of Administrative Services.)

From these meetings, the initial version of the Job Analysis Survey (JAS) began to take shape. (A complete copy of the initial questionnaire is contained in Appendix B.) The questionnaire was divided into three sections. The first section requested a limited amount of personal information about the respondent. Data elements were included that would be helpful in explaining variations in job content that might eventually come to light. The second section, consisting of two parts, dealt with job activities. The first part asked the respondent to apportion his job time, in percentages, among six major clusters of tasks. These clusters were based loosely on the nine objectives contained in the SREB framework. The second part subdivided the six clusters and asked the respondent to distribute his job time among 31 broadly defined tasks. These tasks were not derived from actual analyses of DPS jobs but were inferred from agency job descriptions and from illustrative material developed by participants in the SREB symposia. For the six clusters and the 31 tasks, the respondents were also asked to designate, using a five-point scale, the amount of discretion they were permitted to exercise in carrying out the tasks. In the last section of the questionnaire, the respondents were asked for an overall assessment of the importance and helpfulness of their job. An attempt was also made to measure the worker's influence as reflected by the scope and intensity of personal contacts required by the job.

Initial Results

From January through April 1975 we administered the first version of the JAS to 273 employees in 17 counties and in the central office in Montgomery. This stratified random sample was drawn so as to include workers from each geographic area of the state and from each of the five categories of county departments. (All 67 county departments are categorized, by size, on the basis of county-client population. This, in turn, determines the size of the work force in each county.)

The data collection yielded some useful preliminary findings. Based on similarities in activity, we consolidated several different job classifications into single classes. The instrument had some major shortcomings, however. First, the tasks statements contained in the survey were not real; that is, they were not actually tasks carried out by workers but were composites assembled on an a priori basis from the sources mentioned earlier. Second, the tasks were not specific enough. As a result, the instrument was not able to differentiate well among the various jobs in the series. Finally, the task cluster labels triggered a certain amount of social conformity among the respondents. Apparently, such words as *clerical, supervision,* and *administration* conveyed surplus meaning to the workers. They reported both approach and avoidance responses because of similarity or disimilarity between the cluster labels and the titles of their jobs.

Consequently, although the data collection in the spring of 1975 had some value, progress was obviously constrained by the instrument. Data had to be extracted manually from the JAS, since it did not have a machine-processible format. Description of certain job classes was difficult because of the inability of the JAS to discriminate within several task clusters. Furthermore, little speculation was possible about the complexities of the tasks because they were not actual tasks and could never be subjected to empirical analysis. Finally, there remained the nagging question of validity in light of the reported problems associated with the task labels.

Revisions in the Instrument

With the aforementioned problems in mind, I set about revising the JAS. (Several interim versions were produced, all resembling the final product. In the interest of brevity, only the final version has been given in Appendix C.) In the first section, the questions dealing with personal information were changed to facilitate machine processing of the data. We converted open-ended questions into ones involving limited responses selected from precoded alternatives. (The Coding and Instruction Booklet containing this information is found in Appendix D.) All variable-length data (for example, name) were given fixed-limit fields. In Part I, we reorganized information about job activity into a sequence of 77 specific task statements. The tasks, grouped into eight clusters, drew heavily from the Florida Task Bank, which had just become available. The task clusters were reviewed by selected workers and key personnel in the Bureau of Administrative Services. Definitions of the clusters and the number of tasks assigned to each may be found in Table 2.2. The number of items contained in each cluster was designed to reflect the emphases revealed through interviews and discussions with DPS personnel as well as the emphasis suggested by the content distribution of the Florida Task Bank. Great care was taken with language. So far as possible, the social desirability cues revealed by the pretests were removed from items and cluster labels. All items were rewritten to make them approximately equal in length and in specificity. With few exceptions, items followed a strict syntax, consisting of a verb, an object, modifiers, and an "in order to" clause. The SREB experience, the Florida project, and the DPS pretests had all shown conclusively that task statements with the "in order to" phrase followed by the purpose of the activity had much more meaning for social service workers.

In Part I, workers were asked to indicate how often they carried out each of the 77 tasks. To respond, they used a five-point scale of frequencies (see Appendix D). In order to enhance interval-scale

TABLE 2.2
Task Clusters in the Job Analysis Survey

Cluster	Definition	Number of Tasks
1. Direct Clinical	Activities relating to the provision of direct assistance and care to clients	28
2. Indirect Clinical	Activities that indirectly result in or lend support to services for clients	8
3. Programming and Directing Work (Self)	Activities relating to the organizing and scheduling of the worker's own activities	5
4. Programming and Directing Work (Others)	Activities relating to the organizing and scheduling of the work of others	7
5. Development (Self)	Activities associated with self-learning and growth as a worker	2
6. Development (Others)	Activities relating to the teaching and training of other workers	5
7. Information Processing	Activities associated with recording and documenting facts about clients, workers, supplies, and agency resources	7
8. Managing Work Units	Activities relating to directing and administering various types of programs and organizations	15

Note: No Analyses of the factor structure of the JAS had yet been made. Items were assigned to these eight clusters purely on the basis of content similarity.

properties, the phraseology of this scale was based on the work of Schriessheim and Schriessheim (1974). Respondents were also asked whether or not each task was a regular part of their job and to reply to this query by selecting the appropriate precoded alternative. All responses were marked in the survey booklet.

Part II asked the respondents to account for the way they spent their time on the job. They did this by distributing their time, expressed in percentages, across the eight task clusters depicted in Table 2.2. They were instructed to use a typical month as a frame of reference. In a second section of this part, respondents indicated the ways in which they received information about how and when to do things in their job. They were to distribute their dependence, expressed in percentages, on three forms of information—written, verbal, and self. In short, it was a measure of discretion.

During the pretests, it had been clearly established that workers could not respond easily to questions measuring discretion at the task or task-cluster level. The process took too long, and respondents stated that the discriminations were too fine to make accurately. Therefore, in the final version of the JAS we included only one measure of discretion, based on the job as a whole.

Part III of the JAS dealt exclusively with measures of a variety of job attributes and with characteristics of the setting in which the work was carried out. It also contains material that enabled the respondent to express his reactions to many aspects of the job situation. The contents of this part of the JAS can best be explained within the context of the extensive research associated with the development of the Job Diagnostic Survey (JDS), of which it is a part. Discussion of the JDS work is deferred until Chapters 4 and 5, where the data from Part III of the JAS are presented.

As can be seen, the pretest resulted in extensive revisions of the Job Analysis Survey. The result was a compact, machine-processible, self-reporting instrument, which could be conveniently administered to workers either individually or in groups. The pretest demonstrated that one person could conveniently provide orientation and answer questions for groups of up to 30 people. Although workers with minimal education (eighth grade or less) had some difficulty, the language level of the instructions, codes, and survey items presented few problems.

Respondents

Sampling Approach

Our chief concern in developing the sample was to make it as representative as possible of the work force in the department within the limitations of time and cost. It was deemed important to cover the range of jobs in the social worker series and to capture the major sources of variation in job duties. The pretest, described earlier in this chapter, had shown that the job activity of incumbents, even within the same classification, could vary considerable from one county to another. As a result, it seemed desirable to sample widely from counties of differing size and location.

In Figure 2.1, the counties included in the sample are depicted on a map of the state of Alabama. Each county is coded for size, from the small, rural counties (category 1) to the urban centers (category 5). Each major geographic area of the state is represented. Departments in population centers, such as Birmingham (Jefferson County) and Mobile (Mobile County), are included along with those from the

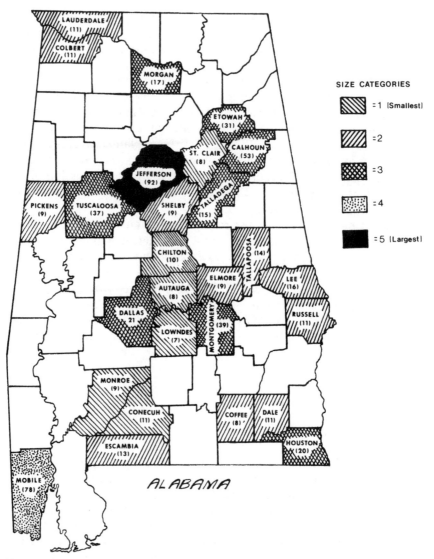

Numbers in parentheses in each county indicate sample size from that unit. The number from Montgomery County does not include 83 state office workers.

FIGURE 2.1. Location of Workers in the Sample

sparsely populated counties of the southern and western part of the state. Counties containing major industries, universities, and military installations were also included in the sample.

In all, 27 county departments were covered, and data were collected from 661 workers. Of these, 578 people worked in the county departments and the remaining 83 worked in various planning and administrative positions in the state office in Montgomery.

At each location, the sampling of workers was carried out through what was basically a stratified random-sampling plan. Each classification within the social worker series was considered a stratum, and every effort was made to sample in proportion to the occurence of that class in the overall work force. The dominant classes in the series, such as Social Worker I, Case Work Reviewer, Eligibility Technician, and Human Services Aide II, were thus emphasized in the sampling. To ensure reliability, classes with small numbers were slightly over-sampled. Within a given classification, we selected workers at random so that each incumbent had an equal likelihood of being chosen. No one was used who had not worked in a particular position for at least six months.

Administrative Procedures

All questionnaires were administered in group sessions. The size of the group depended mainly on logistical constraints, such as room capacity; but some groups had as many as 50 people. Typically, two monitors were present to supervise the administration of the instruments.

All sessions were preceded by a carefully standardized briefing, which covered the purposes of the research and the uses to which the data would be put. Every worker was given an opportunity to refuse to participate or to withhold information, including personal data, selectively. Any questions or problems were dealt with quickly by the monitors. Workers were given assistance but never directions.

Once a questionnaire was completed, a process that averaged one and a half hours, it was given to a monitor, sealed in a packet, and sent to the project staff for data processing. No raw data or questionnaires were seen by agency managers.

Sample Characteristics

The distribution of positions held by the workers in the sample is depicted in Table 2.3. The distribution across the classifications for the entire department is also shown in that table. The 661 respondents in the sample make up 25 percent of the workers in the social worker series. (The six food assistance workers were not part of the social worker series. These were new positions, included in the sample to learn more about the nature of the work activity.) As the table indicates, the strata in the sample are roughly proportionate to their incidence in the population.

TABLE 2.3
Job Composition of the Sample

Classification	Number in Department[a]	Percentage in Department[b]	Number in Sample	Percentage in Sample[b]
Human Services Aide I	8	0.30	4	0.6
Human Services Aide II	221	8.00	39	6.0
Human Services Aide III	16	0.60	11	1.7
Food Assistance Field Agent	9	0.30	4	0.6
Food Assistance Field Supervisor	1	0.04	1	0.1
Public Assistance Eligibility Technician	351	13.00	65	10.0
Activity Program Specialist	2	0.08	1	0.1
Casework Reviewer	369	14.00	124	19.0
Social Worker I	1,416	53.00	276	42.0
Social Worker II	58	2.00	24	3.6
Casework Supervisor	73	3.00	37	5.6
Food Assistance Administrator I	1	0.04	1	0.1
Director I	23	0.80	3	0.4
Director II	33	1.00	14	2.0
Director III	12	0.40	10	1.5
Director IV	1	0.04	1	0.1
Director V	1	0.04	1	0.1
Welfare Administrator I	8	0.30	6	0.9
Welfare Administrator II	6	0.20	4	0.6
Welfare Supervisor I	28	1.00	12	1.8
Welfare Supervisor II	34	1.00	14	2.0
Welfare Supervisor III	13	0.50	8	1.2
Emergency Welfare Supervisor	1	0.04	1	0.1
Total	2,685	100.0	661	100.0

[a]As of March 1976.

[b]Totals may not be exact because of rounding.

In addition to the representativeness of the positions and locations sampled, there are other indications that the sample is a good one. It accurately reflects the ethnic and sexual composition of the work force. As in many social service departments throughout the country, the bulk of the workers (86 percent) are women. In the sample, 563 respondents (85 percent) are women. There are few Hispanics or Orientals in the state, and none are employed in the social worker series. Fourteen percent of the sample is black, however, an exact duplicate of the black population in the departmental work force.

In short, the care taken to generate the sample seems to have paid off. It reflects a good diversity of county location and size. The classification strata are roughly proportionate to the population. Finally, the important demographic characteristics of the overall work force are matched exactly by those of the sample.

Additional Characteristics

Respondents in the sample span a wide range of age—from 20 to 74 years. Most, however, are relatively young. The average age is 36.1 years, but half the people are 32 years of age or younger. There is no significant difference in age between the male and female respondents in the sample ($p < .05$).

Given the wide range of jobs reflected in the sample, we expected to find a broad spectrum of educational backgrounds. Such is indeed the case. The educational background of the incumbents in each of the classifications is depicted in Table 2.4. The respondents are a relatively well-educated group of people. Almost 84 percent of the people have at least a baccalaureate degree. Many of the workers have specialized training in social work. Eighty-seven people (13 percent) have the BSW degree and 106 workers (16 percent) have earned the MSW degree. The next most prevalent major is sociology; 118 workers (18 percent) designated this as their undergraduate major. A background in education accounts for the educational orientation of 77 workers (12 percent). The paraprofessional group, the Human Services Aides, has a predictably low education level because of the low entry qualifications for the position. Sixteen of the aides, however, have some college experience. As one moves up the ladder, the familiar link with educational credentials becomes quite strong. In the sample, all workers above the level of Social Worker II have at least some graduate training.

There is no difference in the average educational level of male and female workers, but a decided difference exists between blacks and whites. Eighty-eight percent of the white workers have at least a baccalaureate degree, while only 52 percent of the black workers have reached this level. This situation is rapidly changing in the state. At this writing, enrollment figures at the major graduate institution in Alabama indicate that 24 percent of the undergraduate majors and 19 percent of the graduate students in social work are black.

The workers in the sample are mostly native Alabamians. Of those who have been to college, 64 percent attended schools within the state. Given the relatively young age of most of the respondents, the dates of graduation are not surprising. Almost half the respondents in the sample earned their most recent degree within five years of the time they participated in the study. Eighty-seven percent of those with the BSW degree were graduated within the same recent five-year period. This reflects the relative newness of many of the BSW programs within the state.[3]

The sample more than adequately covers the range of programs administered by the agency, as can be seen in Table 2.5. A sizable

TABLE 2.4
Educational Level of Respondents

Series Classification	Less than Twelfth Grade	High School or G.E.D.	Some College	A.A. Degree	Bachelor's Degree	BSW Degree	Some Graduate Work	MSW Degree	Total
Human Services Aide	10[a]	28	14	1			1		54
Food Assistance Field Agent			2		2				4
Food Assistance Field Supervisor								1	1
Public Assistance Eligibility Technician		21	26	5	11		2		65
Program Activity Specialist					1				1
Casework Reviewer	1				97	9	13	4	124
Social Worker I					162	73	27	14	276
Social Worker II					1	5	4	14	24
Casework Supervisor					3		9	25	37
Food Assistance Administrator			1						1
Director I, II							12	5	17
Director III							3	7	10
Director IV							1		1
Director V								1	1
Welfare Administrator I, II							2	8	10
Welfare Supervisor I							2	10	12
Welfare Supervisor II							1	13	14
Welfare Supervisor III							3	5	8
Emergency Welfare Supervisor							1		1
Total	11	49	43	6	277	87	81	107	661

Note: Numbers are frequencies.

TABLE 2.5
Program Assignments of Respondents

Program Area	Number
Services	
Adult	84
Aid to Families with Dependent Children (AFDC)	91
Child Welfare	43
Combination[a]	104
Day Care	7
Contract	9
Emergency Welfare	3
Income Maintenance	
Adult	11
AFDC	90
Combination[b]	34
Food Assistance	104
Medical Care	17
Child Support	12
Work Incentive (WIN)	12
Staff Development	5
Unassigned	35
Total	661

[a]Involves any combination of Adult, Child Welfare, or AFDC.

[b]Involves any combination of financial assistance programs, such as state supplementation, AFDC, OAP.

number of respondents (52 percent) were assigned to the various service programs of the department. The agency's extensive involvement in assistance payments is underscored by the 135 workers (20 percent) who are part of the different income maintenance programs. Earlier in the chapter, the agency's expansion into food-related programs was noted. The sample reflects this growth in that 104 people (16 percent) are assigned to various food assistance programs. Almost 3 percent of the respondents are attached to the Medical Care Division of the agency, and 12 people (2 percent) are part of the Work Incentive (WIN) program. Only a small group of workers (5 percent) were unassigned at the time of the study.

Because of the wide range in respondents' ages, we also expected a high degree of variability in tenure on the job and with the agency. This is indeed the case, as the data in Table 2.6 show. When the data were gathered, some workers had been on the job for as little as six months, while others had been in their jobs for over 30 years. This latter group is obviously a small minority, since the average tenure on the job is only 3.6 years. In fact, 71 percent of the respondents had been in their present positions for three years or less when the study

TABLE 2.6
Work Tenure of Respondents

Series Classification	Number	Tenure (years)[a]	
		On Job	With Agency
Human Services Aides	54	2.2	3.7
Food Assistance Field Agent	4	8.0	8.0
Food Assistance Field Supervisor	1	2.0	8.0
Public Assistance Eligibility Technician	65	3.7	5.2
Activity Program Specialist	1	2.0	2.0
Casework Reviewer	124	4.3	4.9
Social Worker I	276	3.1	3.4
Social Worker II	24	5.5	8.1
Casework Supervisor	37	5.1	14.5
Food Assistance Administrator I	1	2.0	13.0
Director I, II	17	6.8	23.1
Director III	10	8.6	20.5
Director IV	1	32.0	43.0
Director V	1	5.0	22.0
Welfare Administrator I, II	10	8.3	19.2
Welfare Supervisor I	12	4.2	9.7
Welfare Supervisor II	14	3.5	10.0
Welfare Supervisor III	8	3.5	15.9
Emergency Welfare Supervisor	1	14.0	19.0
Total	661	3.6	7.3

[a]All tenure figures are arithmetic means.

was carried out. The data about tenure with the agency also reflect this positive skewness. Although the average time with the department, 7.3 years, is significantly higher, long-term employees are in the minority and are usually at the higher levels of the social worker series (that is, Case Work Supervisor or above). Fifty percent of the respondents have been with the agency for a period of four years or less. An inspection of the paired tenure figures for each position clearly suggests that, at the lower levels of the series, most respondents have been on the job only slightly less time than their tenure with the agency. In other words, for many of these people it is their first job with the agency. Given the average ages of the people in these groups, it seemed likely that they had been employed elsewhere before. (The average ages for the respondents in the Aide, Eligibility Technician, Reviewer, and Social Worker I positions were 43.4, 36.2, and 30.1 years, respectively.) The impression created by these data is one of relatively high turnover in these positions.[4]

SUMMARY

It should be clear at this point that great care was taken to assemble a representative group of respondents from whom to collect information. The foregoing summary of characteristics should suggest that this was, in large measure, achieved. As samples go, this one is of more than adequate size. Furthermore, it represents a good cross section of the social workers in the department with regard to age, race, sex, educational level, program, and position. As the chapter has demonstrated, the survey instrument, the JAS, was the product of years of evolution and the efforts of several investigators working in a collaborative fashion. The heart of the JAS is, of course, the material dealing with task activity and job attributes. The care taken with the sampling plan and data collection procedures was done only to make the job information as meaningful as possible. The next chapter describes in detail how the data from this important section of the survey were reduced, analyzed, and interpreted.

NOTES

1. For a complete description of this undertaking, the reader should consult the original series of project reports (U.S. Department of Health, Education and Welfare 1971, 1974; Katzell, Korman, and Levine 1971; Olmstead 1973.)

2. A full treatment of this effort cannot be given in this book. For more details, see Austin (1977) and the two final reports for the project (Office of Career Planning and Curriculum Development for the Human Services 1975a, 1975b).

3. In this respect, Alabama is typical of most of the states. The reader should remember that the first undergraduate BSW program accreditations did not occur until July 1974 (Baer and Federico 1977).

4. Data on turnover or separation were not available for the time period covered by this study. An extensive review of worker mobility by Katzell, Korman, and Levine (1971) suggests that high turnover would not be unusual among workers of this kind. Data from studies covering thousands of service and public assistance workers indicate annual turnover rates ranging from 22 to 50 percent.

3
Social Work Practice: Analysis and Findings

THE HIERARCHICAL GROUPING PROCEDURE

A major objective of the research was to produce a concise depiction of the activities carried out by the workers in the department. Obviously, something better than a listing of the 77 tasks in the JAS was in order; the task material had to be reduced to a more manageable descriptive framework.

To get this done, we used the hierarchical grouping procedure, as described by Ward and Hook (1963). This technique permits one to take a number of elements—for example, people, items, and tests—and combine them into groups based on their similarity to one another. Using a criterion measure of some kind, usually a profile, all elements in a sample are compared. The two with the most similar profiles are combined into a group. Groups are formed in an iterative fashion until, at the end, all sample elements are collapsed into a single group. It is obvious that this is the least precise solution, since the final single group will contain many elements with dissimilar profiles. The ideal solution is assumed to lie somewhere between the starting point, where there are as many groups as there are sample elements, and the final formation of a single group. To determine this, a measure of error is calculated at each step in the grouping sequence. This is usually a measure of variability reflecting the differences among the profile points of the elements within the various groups. A large jump in the error measure from one stage to the next indicates that the groups just formed contain elements that are too dissimilar, and the groupings just prior to the jump are chosen as the ideal solution.

Development of Task Clusters

In the first stage of the analysis of the task data, we concentrated on trying to identify the dimensions underlying the 77 task statements in the JAS. To begin this process, a profile was constructed for each statement. The profile consisted of the standard scores of all 661 respondents for that item.[1] We compared each pair of profiles and, using the error criterion described earlier, recombined the tasks into the fewest possible homogeneous clusters. (The procedure is roughly analogous to factor analysis but avoids some of the interpretive difficulties associated with that process.) Each cluster thus consisted of those items that behaved the same way, that is, were highly correlated, across the sample of workers. Since these clusters were composites of a number of tasks, they were much more stable than any single task and were thus a far better vehicle for describing the similarities and differences among respondents and their jobs.

Twelve clusters emerged from the analysis. These dimensions of practice are summarized in Table 3.1. The table contains a definition of each cluster, the number of tasks contributing to its makeup, and its internal consistency reliability. As expected, some clusters contain more items than others. (A listing of the tasks in each cluster can be found in Appendix E.) The largest cluster, Employee Supervision, consists of 12 task statements. Three others, Counseling, Personal Care, and Program Management, have eight items. The smallest clusters, Compiling Information and General Care Management, each have

TABLE 3.1
Major Task Clusters in the Job Analysis Survey

---

1. Linkage: Connecting clients with resources, opportunities, and services; evaluating and licensing resources; trying to improve service to clients.
   (7 items) $r_{tt} = .78$[a]

2. Teaching: Teaching clients skills (e.g., money management, personal hygiene, literacy, food preparation) and behaviors (e.g., taking job interviews, working in a group).
   (6 items) $r_{tt} = .88$

3. Counseling, Informing: Providing information to clients; defining needs; casefinding; explaining programs; advising clients; relieving anxiety; choosing courses of action.
   (8 items) $r_{tt} = .92$

4. Personal Care: Providing direct, tangible sercies to clients (e.g., assisting in dressing, carrying out housekeeping, preparing meals, giving medicines) of a maintenance or custodial nature.
   (8 items) $r_{tt} = .94$

(*continued*)

TABLE 3.1 Continued

5. Case Management (Specific): Preparing records, schedules, and files to plan work around *specific* clients; carrying out intake; determining eligibility for services or public assistance.
   (7 items) r_{tt} = .91

6. Compiling Information: Processing numerical and statistical information; making listings; carrying out studies for costing, reimbursement, planning purposes.
   (3 items) r_{tt} = .61

7. External Relations: Meeting with citizens or client groups; designing and conducting opinion surveys; gathering support for programs; making speeches and presentations.
   (6 items) r_{tt} = .80

8. Management of Tangibles: Taking care of physical components of an operation (e.g., inventory control, ordering supplies, transporting property, inspecting facilities, maintaining security).
   (4 items) r_{tt} = .81

9. Program Management: Planning details of new programs; designing training; reviewing and preparing budgets; writing policy; conducting meetings; recruiting and screening personnel.
   (8 items) r_{tt} = .89

10. Employee Supervision: Evaluating employee performance; preparing work schedules; teaching workers; giving advice with worker problems; orienting new workers; assigning cases to workers.
    (12 items) r_{tt} = .98

11. Case Management (General): Reviewing policies and procedures applicable to *many* clients; planning general work activities; discussing program operations with co-workers.
    (3 items) r_{tt} = .57

12. Paper Flow: Using standard forms to carry out routine procedures (e.g., processing vouchers, filling out time sheets, dictating and proofreading correspondence and case records).
    (4 items) r_{tt} = .57

[a]Kuder-Richardson (KR_{20}) coefficient of internal consistency, roughly equivalent to the average of all possible pairs of item intercorrelations within a given cluster.

three tasks in them. Only one task, which involves the transportation of clients (Part I, Task 6), was not included in the groupings. Because it was performed so infrequently, it could not be assigned to a cluster and was deleted from the analysis. Eight of the twelve clusters have reliability coefficients of .80 or greater. This is certainly acceptable reliability. Since each cluster is really a blend of tasks of slightly different content, item intercorrelations within a cluster should not be too high or the true diversity of the work content would be lost in the pursuit of internal consistency. The lowest reliabilities are associated with the clusters that contain only a few items (clusters 11 and 12). Adding items with equivalent content would increase the internal consistency of these clusters. This was done in subsequent versions of the Job Analysis Survey.

Establishing Cluster Relationships

An inspection of the content underlying the various dimensions (clusters) shows them to be diverse. Since they constitute areas of practice content, it is important to understand them more completely. It seems particularly useful to find out which dimensions group together on the job and which do not. This information would add more clarity and detail to any discussion of the generalist-specialist continuum.

An obvious approach was to do an analysis of the intercorrelations among the various clusters. Accordingly, we generated a 12 × 12 matrix of intercorrelations, shown in Table 3.2. Although the intercorrelations may be confusing at first, some distinct patterns are present. First, there is a group of related clusters involving Personal Care, Teaching, Counseling, and Linkage. These clusters seem to be a configuration centering on what many practitioners have called direct practice—activities or interventions that involve clients directly. Another grouping involves clusters dealing with External Relations, Program Management, Supervision, Management of Tangibles, and Compiling Information. This broad configuration, generally concerned with management and administration, comes close to the traditional notion of indirect practice—activities done on behalf of clients but not involving them directly in the process. To clarify the nature of these two configurations, see Table 3.3.

In the table we have rearranged the clusters into two major divisions (broken lines). The first column lists the average correlation of each of the twelve clusters with the five that make up the direct practice configuration. The second column shows the average correlation with the six clusters in the indirect practice configuration. The pattern is now much clearer. Clusters *within* each configuration correlate positively with each other but are independent or negatively correlated with clusters in the other configuration. Two clusters seem to be exceptions to this pattern. Paper Flow (cluster 12) has positive correlations with both major configurations. At this point, it is being viewed as an adjunct area to both modes of practice. (This interpretation should be viewed with some caution, however, because this cluster has a relatively low reliability coefficient. Its correlation pat-

TABLE 3.2
Matrix of Intercorrelations among Various Practice Clusters

	Linkage	Teaching	Counseling, Informing	Personal Care	Case Management (Specific)	Compiling Information	External Relations	Management of Tangibles	Program Management	Employee Supervision	Case Management (General)	Paper Flow
Linkage		.54	.67	.06	.32	.35	.06	-.05	-.08	-.07	.19	.31
Teaching			.45	.65	.15	-.04	-.12	-.11	-.29	-.30	-.11	.15
Counseling, Informing				-.02	.66	-.03	-.18	-.16	-.40	-.41	.07	.37
Personal Care					-.21	-.11	-.09	-.02	-.14	-.15	-.20	-.13
Case Management (Specific)						-.28	-.25	-.21	-.55	-.55	.16	.44
Compiling Information							.48	.34	.64	.53	.36	.11
External Relations								.31	.55	.75	.22	.21
Management of Tangibles									.58	.45	.18	.06
Program Management										.75	.29	.00
Employee Supervision											.38	-.01
Case Management (General)												.28
Paper Flow												

Note: Numbers are Pearson product-moment correlations (*r*). Correlations greater than ±.08 are significantly different from zero (*p* < .05).

TABLE 3.3
Relationships between Direct and Indirect Practice

Clusters	Average Correlation with Direct Practice	Average Correlation with Indirect Practice
1. Linkage	.40	.07
2. Teaching	.45	-.16
3. Counseling, Informing	.44	-.18
4. Personal Care	.12	-.12
5. Case Management (Specific)	.23	-.28
6. Compiling Information	.02	.47
7. External Relations	-.12	.46
8. Management of Tangibles	-.11	.37
9. Program Management	-.29	.56
10. Employee Supervision	-.30	.52
11. Case Management (General)	.02	.34
12. Paper Flow	.23	.11

Note: Numbers are Pearson product-moment correlations (r).

tern may thus be an artifact, not a result of inherent relationships among tasks.) Cluster 4, Personal Care, does not correlate strongly with either configuration. An extremely reliable cluster, it is highly correlated ($r = .65$) with Teaching and has consistenly negative correlations with the indirect practice clusters. For these reasons, we have placed it within the direct practice configuration.

A Model of Practice

The geometry of a model of practice suggested by the data is presented visually in Figure 3.1. This depiction is based on some conventional practices associated with data displays involving correlation coefficients. In the figure, each of the original 12 clusters is represented by a sphere. The spheres overlap with one another to varying degrees. The overlap between any two spheres in proportionate to their common variance. (Common variance, or communality, is computed by squaring the correlation between two variables.) Using this technique, we have represented the two major practice configurations by

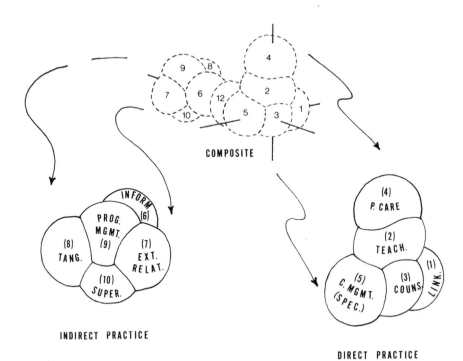

FIGURE 3.1. A Model of Practice

a cluster of tightly grouped spheres. These are seen on the right and left sides of the figure. As Table 3.3 showed, the two configurations are relatively independent of each other; the average correlation across configurations is −.13. In correlation, such independence is traditionally depicted by placing objects in perpendicular planes. Accordingly, in the composite model shown in the center of the figure, the planes in which the two configurations lie are at right angles to each other.

In short, the data clearly suggest two major areas of practice, with a number of components in each. These two areas are unrelated to each other. This means that a person involved in direct practice activities is not very likely to be engaged in indirect services. Given the nature of the department in which the data were gathered, this is not surprising. The agency has a large staff of people involved in the delivery of a wide variety of direct services to clients. Approximately 400 members of the sample fall into this category. There is also a large work force of supervisory and management personnel. About 250 respondents hold these kinds of positions. Thus, the practice configuration directly reflects the ways in which the labor is divided in the department. The next step in the analysis was to investigate this further by using the JAS to describe the job patterns in the department.

THE DEVELOPMENT OF JOB CLUSTERS

The Subgrouping Procedure

To produce this information, we again used the hierarchical grouping procedure. This time, we constructed profiles for every respondent in the sample. The frequency scores for all items in each cluster were totaled for each worker. These totals were then converted to a distribution of 661 Z-scores. (This operation permits one to make direct comparison between scales and to construct profiles with a common metric.) This was done for each of the 12 clusters. Each respondent's JAS scores were thus converted into a 12-point profile expressed in Z-score form. These standardized profiles were the data on which the next hierarchical grouping was carried out.

Basically, the subgrouping procedure compared the profiles of all 661 workers. It formed groups by placing workers with similar profiles together. Thus, each group consisted of those workers whose job profiles were most like those within the group and least like those in other groups. Twenty groups of workers were formed by the subgrouping procedure. Table 3.4 summarizes the various job classifications contained in each group. It is clear that the groups vary greatly in size. The smallest (group 3) has 4 people, while the largest (group 6) consists of 68 respondents.

The results of the second subgrouping are impressive. The analysis strongly suggests that the JAS is able to capture much of the work content of the jobs. If this were not so, there would be little correspondence between the job classifications and the composition of the groups. Table 3.4 shows that the correspondence is very good. Groups 1, 2, and 3 encompass 85 percent of all the Human Services Aides. Almost all the Eligibility Technicians can be found in 8 of the 20 groups. With very few exceptions, all management and supervisory personnel (classes above the level of Social Worker II) can be found in just 7 of the groups.

There are exceptions, however, to this pattern of consistency. Rather than negating the JAS, the exceptional patterns reinforce its content validity. As stated earlier, an important reason for doing the research was to identify the job classes that contained diverse and inconsistent patterns of worker activity. For years, the Reviewer classification was suspected to be one of these. This class has a broad definition of work and does not require any graduate training. As a result, it had long been used as a place to assign workers with supervisory and management skills who did not have any prospects for graduate education. At the time of the study, almost 370 workers (14 percent of the work force) had been assigned to this classification. Often,

TABLE 3.4
Distribution of Classifications in Various Job Groups

Classification											Job Groups[a]										
	1	2	3	5	8	9	10	11	6	7	12	13	14	17	19	4	15	16	20	18	Total
Human Services Aide I		3																		1	4
Human Services Aide II	13	22	2																	2	39
Human Services Aide III	2	1	1																	3	11
Food Assistance Field Agent														3						1	4
Food Assistance Field Supervisor																				1	1
Public Assistance Eligibility Technician				16	15	7	13	6	1	1	3				1					2	65
Activity Program Specialist		1																			1
Casework Reviewer			1	23	3	17	1	12	1	1	1	1	20	9		4	16	3	11	4	124
Social Worker I				1	24	33	34	11	60	35	11	40			1					3	276
Social Worker II							1		6	9	3	4								2	24
Casework Supervisor													14	3			10	1	7	2	37
Food Assistance Administrator I																					1
Director I																		3			3
Director II																	1	10	1	2	14
Director III																		9		1	10
Director IV																		1			1
Director V																		1			1
Welfare Administrator I														1		1				5	6
Welfare Administrator II														1		1	1			1	4
Welfare Supervisor I					1		1						1	1		1	1			8	12
Welfare Supervisor II													1	1	1	1	1		2	7	14
Welfare Supervisor III													2			1	2			3	8
Emergency Welfare Supervisor																		1			1
Total	15	27	4	40	43	57	50	29	68	45	18	45	40	19	25	8	31	29	22	46	661

[a]Groups are listed out of sequence to facilitate comparisons.

workers with widely disparate duties would be put into this classification because of its broad and somewhat nebulous definition. As Table 3.4 shows, workers in this classification can be found in 14 of the 20 job groups. A somewhat similar situation exists with the Social Worker I classification. Workers in this job category can be found in 11 groups. This reflects the fact that the Social Worker I was used both for income maintenance functions (eligibility determination) and for the delivery of social services. The subgroupings give evidence of this diversity in job functions.

The JAS was thus able to pick up the "noise" that existed in the classification system. Given the diversity of programs administered by the department and the range of settings in which it operated, this inconsistency is acceptable. Some modifications were in order, however. Some steps taken by the department to correct the situation will be described in later chapters.

Formation of Job Families

The profiles of each of the 20 groups of workers are very distinct because of the criteria built into the subgrouping procedure. An inspection of the profiles indicates, however, that many of the groups seem to be variations of a more limited set of generic profiles of job

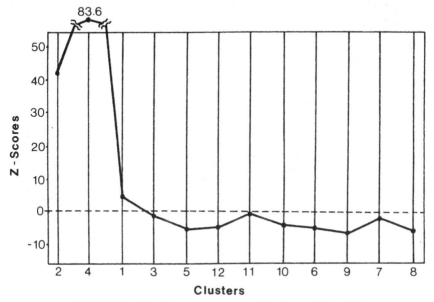

FIGURE 3.2. Human Services Workers (N = 46)

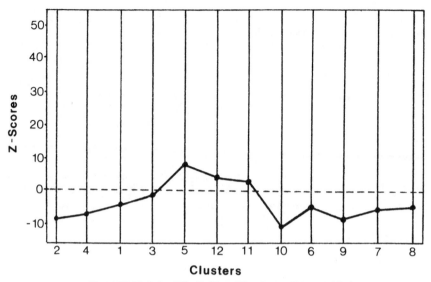

FIGURE 3.3. Eligibility Workers (N = 219)

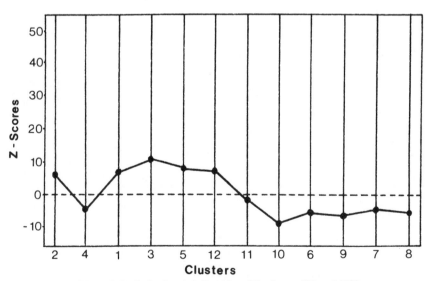

FIGURE 3.4. Social Service Workers (N = 176)

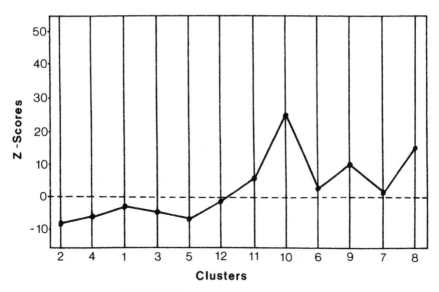

FIGURE 3.5. Supervisors (N = 84)

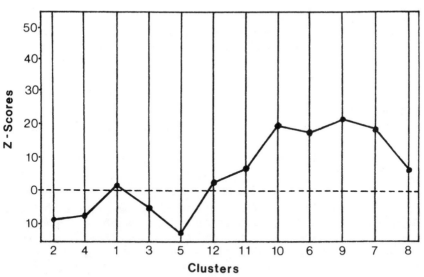

Key: 2-Teaching; 4-Personal Care; 1-Linkage; 3-Counseling, Informing; 5-case Management (Specific); 12-Paper Flow; 11-Case Management (General); 10-Employee Supervision; 6-Compiling Information; 9-Program Management; 7-External Relations; 8-Management of Tangibles

FIGURE 3.6 Administrators (N = 90)

families. We have identified five such basic families and have constructed a composite profile for each. The composite for a given job family was constructed by computing a weighted average for each profile point (cluster). The scores averaged were the profile scores for those groups of the original 20 that were assigned to the job family, and the weights were based on the number of workers in each group so assigned. The composite profiles are shown in Figures 3.2 through 3.6.

Before describing the characteristics of the various job families, some comments about interpretation of the figures are in order. Each profile is basically a two-dimensional display. Along the bottom, the 12 dimensions that emerged from the first hierarchical analysis are listed. Each dimension represents a cluster of JAS items. Along the left-hand border, divisions are made in Z-score units. The broken line across the figure corresponds to a Z-score of 0.00. A point plotted at this level would correspond to the average of the entire sample of respondents. Points below the line are levels that are below average for the sample. Thus a point plotted at a Z-score of -2.5 would represent a level of involvement that is two and a half standard deviations below the mean of the respondents. By the same token, points plotted above the line indicate a higher than average involvement in that cluster. Thus, the peaks and valleys of the profiles represent high and low involvement in the tasks represented by the corresponding clusters.

Paraprofessionals

The paraprofessional job family is composed of the original job groups 1 through 3. It contains a total of 46 workers. They are part of the adult services program, and most of them (89 percent) are used as homemakers providing services to clients in their own homes. Figure 3.2 shows an extremely high loading in the Personal Care cluster, as one would expect. (A listing of tasks in each cluster is given in Appendix E.) In fact, this group of workers is the only one that provides this type of tangible, direct service. Frequent contact with clients, over extended periods of time, permits them to do a large amount of teaching, particularly around specific skills. As a result, the Teaching component of their jobs is very high. As mentioned earlier, the Personal Care cluster did not intercorrelate very highly with any other cluster in the Direct Practice configuration except for Teaching. The paraprofessional family accounts for this pattern, since these two clusters essentially define that family's jobs.

Since the paraprofessionals are able to see clients in the home, they often serve as a bridge or link between clients and the additional services they need. Hence, the Linkage component is above the average of the rest of the sample. In short, these workers maintain a frequent prolonged contact with clients on a highly interpersonal level.

The paraprofessionals hold the entry-level positions in the social worker series. As a group, they fit the classic demographic pattern of paraprofessionals in the human services (U.S. Department of Health, Education and Welfare 1974). All are female, and most are black. Almost three-fourths of the group has a high school education or less. The average paraprofessional is 36 years old, but the age range is wide—from 22 to 69 years.

Eligibility Workers

Figure 3.3 depicts another predictable division of labor in public welfare practice. As the title Eligibility Worker implies, most of the workers in this family are involved in the determination of eligibility for the wide range of programs offered by the department, including social services, food stamps, and the public assistance program. This family of workers is the largest; it contains 219 employees and comprises 33 percent of the sample in the study. It was formed by combining job groups 5, 8, 9, 10, and 11.

As the profile shows, this group of workers is involved primarily with those activities subsumed under Case Management, both general and specific. The profile is also elevated for Paper Flow. The data thus confirm the basic cognitive nature of the jobs in this family and the fact that they require a good deal of paperwork. The profile also indicates that there is little involvement in direct services, such as Teaching, Linkage, and Counseling. Workers in this family also have few Supervision or Program Management responsibilities.

Three job classes account for the bulk of the workers in this family. Most (50 percent) are in the Social Worker I class, 26 percent are Eligibility Technicians, and the remainder (15 percent) are Reviewers. Given the nature of these jobs (see Appendix A), it is not surprising to find Reviewers and Technicians in this family. It might seem strange, however, for social workers to be carrying out the eligibility functions in a welfare department. Screening for eligibility is one of those paradoxes of modern public welfare systems: accountability has to be maintained and, at the same time, a climate of service needs to be created. Furthermore, this type of initial client contact permits skilled workers to assess the need for various services. In recognition of this difficult role, some months prior to the study, the department started assigning social workers to these tasks.

Most of the workers in this family (73 percent) are assigned to various income maintenance programs. Forty-three percent are in the Aid to Families with Dependent Children (AFDC) program, but a substantial number (28 percent) are assigned to food assistance. Very few of these workers are found in the state office in Montgomery; most (90 percent) are deployed in the various county departments throughout the state .

Workers in this family have typically been to college. Eighty percent have at least a bachelor's degree. Fourteen percent have majored in social work and have the BSW degree. Although 15 percent have taken some graduate courses, only a few (4 percent) have completed work for the MSW. This job family is an exact replica of the departmental work force with respect to sexual and racial composition. Fourteen percent of the workers are black, and 85 percent are women. Like the paraprofessional group, the age range is large. The average worker in this family is 33.4 years old.

Social Service Workers

This family of 197 workers was formed by combining job groups 6, 7, 12, and 13. The group closely fits the traditional image of the social service provider. As Figure 3.4 shows, the profile for this group has a high loading on the Teaching, Linkage, and Counseling dimensions. This pattern is consistent with the direct service orientation of the workers in this family. They differ from the paraprofessionals, however, in that the Personal Care component is low. Much of their service involves exchanging information and providing advice and guidance to clients. In this family, the interpersonal and the cognitive components are both high. Their practice, however, is carried out within an organizational context. In keeping with this fact, the profile reflects a heavy involvement in the case planning and paperwork required by contemporary agency operations. Consequently, Case Management (Specific) and Paper Flow scores are high. Like the previous two groups, these workers have little involvement in Program Management and Supervison.

It is thus consistent that almost all the workers in this family (96 percent) are to be found in either the Social Worker I or Social Worker II class. Most of them provide direct services to adults, families, and children. Almost without exception, they are deployed at the county level. They work in the categorical services, such as adult services (12 percent), AFDC services (36 percent), and child welfare services (15 percent), and in a number of combined service programs (23 percent). From the standpoint of work activities, this is a very homogeneous family of workers.

It is also a relatively well-educated group. Ninety-four percent of the people have at least a bachelor's degree. One-fourth have the BSW, and 13 percent have received the MSW degree. This level of education is consistent with the employment requirements of the department; the social worker classes require at least a bachelor's degree for consideration. Like the groups previously described, the bulk of the workers in this job family (87 percent) are women. Eleven percent of the workers are black. The now-familiar wide range in ages is also present, but these workers tend to be somewhat younger than those in the previous two families. The average age is only 29.8 years.

Supervisors

The fourth major group of workers consists of job groups 14, 17, and 19. This group represents a shift into indirect practice. Almost all its members have heavy responsibilities in Supervision. This concentration of activity is clearly reflected in the profile in Figure 3.5. This group has little to do with the direct provision of services. They specialize in Supervision, Program Management and Management of Tangibles, which includes keeping track of millions of dollars in food stamp inventories. The fact that there is little involvement with the public (External Relations) marks these workers as managers at the unit or program level.

The job classes of the members of this job family are consistent with this middle management thrust; 61 percent are Reviewers, and almost 20 percent are Casework Supervisors. The Reviewers in this group either supervise the food stamp offices attached to the county departments or supervise units of income maintenance workers. As one might expect, the Casework Supervisors in this group provide supervision to the Social Service Workers in the department.

This fourth family is thus clearly seen as the group that provides first-line supervision to service workers, eligibility and income maintenance people, and food stamp personnel throughout the state. Although some are in the state office, most (83 percent) are based in the county departments. Because of the merit-system requirements for most of the jobs in the family, it is a highly educated group; 94 percent have at least a baccalaureate degree. Many of these workers are Reviewers, who are being asked to function in a wide range of management and supervisory capacities. In these cases, experience has been substituted for the graduate training requirement. However, a third of the group has done some graduate work, and 16 percent of the workers have the MSW degree. As with the previous families, most of the workers (83 percent) are women, but the number of minority workers is low (4 percent).[2]

Administrators

The last of the major job families is made up of administrators. This group of 90 workers was formed by combining job groups 4, 15, 16, and 20. The family comprises those workers who can be viewed as the top management of the organization. Like the supervisory group, workers in this family carry out indirect services, but with much less evidence of specialization. As Figure 3.6 clearly shows, there is heavy involvement in a range of management and administrative duties. Since this is a labor-intensive organization, there is the expected emphasis on Supervision. The people being supervised are, for the most part, the program and unit directors in the job family just described.

Administrators are the workers ultimately responsible for the programs of the department (Program Management). They carry out this responsibility at both the state office and county level. In the state office, where 30 percent of these workers are found, they plan and direct the programs that are administered by the counties. Regardless of location, these workers monitor and evaluate the program efforts of the department (Compiling Information). This is the only group that has extensive contact with the general public (External Relations). They are spokespersons and advocates for the department and relate directly to legislators, city and county officials, and special-interest groups.

This group contains all the major county administrators. Twenty-two percent of the workers are County Welfare Directors; this is the only group in which they are to be found. The ubiquitous Reviewer class is also seen again. In fact, with 28 percent of the members, it is the largest single class of workers in the group. Twenty-four percent of the workers are either Welfare Supervisors or Welfare Administrators, and 15 percent are Casework Supervisors.

Workers in this family have the highest level of education. Almost half (46 percent) have the MSW degree, and 19 percent have taken some graduate coursework. Because of the large number of Reviewers in the group, 26 percent have completed only the bachelor's degree. A small proportion of the workers (2 percent) hold the BSW degree. (This group is used by the department in a clinical rather than an administrative capacity. As mentioned earlier, 80 of the 87 BSW graduates in the sample were found in family 2, Eligibility Workers, and family 3, Social Service Workers.) Most of the workers in this group (80 percent) are women, and 5 percent are blacks.

Earlier in the chapter we discussed the relationship between the 20 derived job groups and the existing departmental job classifications.

As can be seen by looking again at Table 3.4, the two schema correspond rather well. When the family groupings are used, the fit is even better. Table 3.5 has been constructed to show the relationship between the job classes and the five families. Only 19 of the 20 job groups have been assigned to a family. Group 18, with 46 workers, did not fit in with any other group. It is a diverse mixture of job classes (see Table 3.4) and is not distinguished by any task dimension. The majority of its members (63 percent) work in the state office. Most of the workers in the sample (92 percent) can be assigned to both a classification and a family. For the most part, the job classifications dovetail neatly into the job families. The Casework Reviewer and the Social Worker I classes are important exceptions to this pattern. For the latter group, the picture is clear: they are either determining eligibility (family 2) or delivering services (family 3). The Reviewer classification does not fit well anywhere. These workers run the gamut from direct to indirect services and are found in three of the five families. Both of these situations were expected, and the data thus confirmed the need for selective modification of a few of the job classifications. These modifications are described in Chapter 6.

FURTHER WORK WITH THE TASK DATA

The first part of this chapter clearly demonstrated that the rather amorphous area of public welfare practice, when subjected to systematic study, can be made to yield up a great deal of order. A configuration of 12 dimensions, generally organized around direct and indirect interventions, emerges from the JAS data analysis. Variations among these dimensions describe rather well what workers in the department did on their jobs.

These findings were most useful in dealing with some of the classification problems. But the department was also interested in applying the findings to questions relating to salaries and to staff development. In order for the data to be used for these purposes, additional analyses had to be carried out. The remainder of this chapter describes those efforts.

Evaluating Compensation

Agency management was interested in seeing how well the existing compensation plan corresponded to the data derived from the JAS. In other words, there was a need to assess the extent to which salary

TABLE 3.5
Distribution of Classifications in Various Job Families

Classification	Paraprofessionals (1)	Eligibility Workers (2)	Social Service Workers (3)	Supervisors (4)	Administrators (5)	Total (number)
			Job Families			
Human Services Aide I	100					3
Human Services Aide II	100					27
Human Services Aide III	50		13	24	13	8
Food Assistance Field Agent				100		3
Food Assistance Field Supervisor	NC[a]					—
Public Assistance Eligibility Technician		91	6	3		63
Activity Program Specialist	100					1
Casework Reviewer		27	1	44	28	120
Social Worker I	.5	46	53	.5		273
Social Worker II		8	92			24
Casework Supervisor				49	51	35
Food Assistance Administrator I					100	1
Director I					100	3
Director II					100	12
Director III					100	9
Director IV					100	1
Director V					100	1
Welfare Administrator I				100		1
Welfare Administrator II				33	67	3
Welfare Supervisor I		50		50		4
Welfare Supervisor II				43	57	7
Welfare Supervisor III				40	60	5
Emergency Welfare Supervisor					100	1
Total						605[b]

Note: Numbers are percentages, except for last column.
[a]Not classified — found in Job Group 18.
[b]Total is decreased by the 46 workers in Job Group 18.

schedules were commensurate with the kind of work employees were being asked to do. To look into this, an extensive analysis was carried out, building on the JAS data base.

Eighteen employees, incumbents in the classes represented in the study (except for the Human Services Aide), were used to provide additional data about the tasks performed in the department. The group consisted of two Public Assistance Eligibility Technicians, five Case Work Reviewers, four Social Workers I, one Social Worker II, one Case Work Supervisor, two Welfare Supervisors I, one Welfare Supervisor II, one County Welfare Director I, and one County Welfare Director II. They were selected by the department personnel officer, using criteria set forth by the U.S. Civil Service Commission (1975). These subject matter experts (SMEs) were all experienced workers with a broad knowledge of the department's programs. They either performed the tasks being evaluated or supervised the people who did.

Measuring Job Attributes

Once the SMEs were briefed on the purposes of the study and the methodology was explained, they were asked to assess a number of attributes of the 77 tasks contained in the JAS. They rated each task in terms of its criticality, the discretion associated with it, the likelihood of serious consequences resulting from its improper execution, and the clarity with which remedial action could be taken.[3] They were asked to rate only the tasks with which they were familiar either as a worker or as a supervisor.

The measurement of the four attributes basically involved the construction of a series of scores at the task, cluster, and job level. First, a rating of the four attributes was obtained for each of the 77 JAS tasks. (Because the SMEs rated only those tasks with which they were familiar, the number of observations varied slightly from task to task.) We then converted these to t-scores to standardize the differing scale units. The use of t-scores avoided the negative numbers usually found with Z-scores and converted the measures of each attribute to a distribution with a mean of 50 and a standard deviation of 10. Each task was now characterized by four attributes expressed in scales with uniform characteristics, which is a necessary precondition for the construction of weighted composite scores.

The next step was to derive attribute scores for the 12 task clusters. We generated these by calculating a weighted average of the t-scores of the tasks in a given cluster. The weights used were the loadings of the tasks in the cluster (see Appendix E).

Finally, a score on each attribute was constructed for each of the job groups. This was done by taking the cluster scores for a given attribute, such as criticality, and calculating a weighted composite score across the 12 clusters, using the following formula:

$$\text{Criticality}_{(\text{Job Group 1})} = \sum_{i=1}^{12} (I_i)A_i$$

where A_i is the attribute score for a given cluster and I_i is the involvement of the job group in that cluster. The involvement score was derived from the frequency data in Part I of the JAS and is analogous to the heights of the profiles depicted in Figures 3.2 through 3.6. The end product of these calculations was a set of four scores, one for each of the job attributes, by which we could characterize the job groups that emerged from the earlier analysis. Table 3.6 contains these data. Each job group and family has been described in terms of the four job attributes.

Salary and Job Importance

As table 3.6 shows, there are distinctly different scores for each group on each attribute. Furthermore, these variations are systematic. There is a decided tendency for the job ratings to increase as one moves from the paraprofessionals (family 1) to the administrators (family 5). One explanation for this might be a halo effect caused by the built-in status differences associated with job titles. It should be pointed out that the original ratings were made at the *task* level. Raters did not know which tasks were associated with clusters, jobs, or families. Thus, the data are more likely to reflect inherent task characteristics than bureaucratic status.

The agency was interested in knowing how well these perceived differences in job characteristics were reflected in the salaries paid to the workers. To shed some light on this, we combined the attributes into an importance index by simply computing the average of the four attribute scores for each job group and family. We correlated this index with the average salaries of the incumbents in each group. (The salary for each group was obtained by combining the fourth step of the pay range for each of the classifications contained in the group.) A Pearson coefficient of .81 was obtained. Given the nature of the scales, one would expect the correlation to be positive, but the high correlation was encouraging indeed. Besides lending credibility to the department's compensation plan, these findings further supported the contention that the Job Analysis Survey was able to capture the salient characteristics of work.

TABLE 3.6

Job Attribute Scores for the JAS Job Groups and Families

Group[a]	N	Criticality	Discretion	Probability of Error	Clarity of Remedy	Importance (composite)
1	15	809.91	893.93	733.25	781.26	804.58
2	27	1062.35	1165.62	968.77	1020.92	1054.42
Family 1	42	972.19	1068.59	884.66	935.33	965.19
5	40	732.85	724.01	685.50	741.49	720.96
8	43	781.84	729.60	712.73	750.1	743.60
9	57	823.24	817.01	780.74	797.11	804.52
10	50	1038.79	1021.30	957.26	1034.05	1012.85
11	29	1075.33	1048.71	1042.76	1063.94	1057.68
Family 2	219	881.20	860.18	824.99	867.17	858.38
6	68	817.21	995.80	868.60	971.78	913.35
7	45	1079.78	1138.73	987.08	1083.70	1072.32
12	18	1289.52	1383.22	1263.52	1371.41	1326.92
13	45	1232.45	1312.53	1153.28	1272.32	1242.89
Family 3	176	1038.82	1152.95	1012.07	1118.36	1082.55
14	40	1052.63	1055.80	1014.09	1105.35	1056.97
17	19	1031.11	1029.78	1017.87	1067.46	1036.55
19	25	1514.56	1445.10	1468.52	1531.14	1489.83
Family 4	84	1185.24	1165.78	1150.19	1223.50	1181.18
15	31	1120.35	1249.96	1192.77	1308.70	1217.95
16	29	1283.56	1567.34	1254.18	1365.35	1367.61
20	20	1378.13	1443.18	1397.55	1497.46	1429.08
Family 5	80	1243.96	1413.32	1266.23	1376.43	1324.98

[a]Job Groups 3, 4, and 18 are not included. Groups 3 and 4, with Ns of 4 and 8, respectively, were considered too small to yield reliable results, and group 18 was considered too diverse to interpret with any clarity.

Formulating Job Requirements

In Chapter 2 we described the range of departmental concerns and expectations that prompted the study. Within that range, it was hoped that the job analysis data could be used to assist in the identification of worker requirements for various jobs in the social worker series. Extensive investment in university education and in-service training programs made it most desirable that departmental decisions about the skills required in its work force be based on a sound framework. With justification, the department did not wish to invest unnecessarily in the development of worker assets that had no bearing on client service or worker effectiveness.

There is much precedent for using job and task analysis data as a springboard for generating worker requirements for jobs (Kleiman and Lounsbury 1978; McCormick 1976). The process is straightforward. Basically, one starts with the job content and, by inference, establishes linkages with some configuration of worker abilities. Most often, the abilities are expressed in terms of knowledge, skills, and values. This inferential leap, though quite subjective, has become an important part of contemporary content validation strategies. Despite widespread use in content validation, however, no standard taxonomy of worker abilities, especially in the human services, has been developed.

A Framework of Abilities

A similar inferential process was carried out with the JAS data. As part of their rating process, the SMEs were asked to review each task and evaluate the extent to which any or all of 47 areas of ability were required for its execution. The framework of abilities used by the raters is presented in Table 3.7.

TABLE 3.7
Knowledge, Skills, and Abilities List Used by Subject Matter Experts

1. Knowledge of eligibility criteria.
2. Knowledge of items and their meanings on standard eligibility forms.
3. Knowledge of interviewing principles and techniques.
4. Knowledge of functions of various assistance agencies.
5. Knowledge of state and federal laws as related to public welfare programs.
6. Knowledge of state and federal laws as related to food stamp program.
7. Knowledge of community resources available and their locations.
8. Knowledge of individual, family, community problems and resources.
9. Knowledge of referral procedures.
10. Knowledge of agency housing standards.
11. Knowledge of the philosophy, history, and development of social welfare programs.
12. Knowledge of the roles of the agency and its relationship to other agencies and governmental programs, including general awareness of broad social problems.
13. Knowledge of current social and economic problems.
14. Knowledge of social problems in relation to family disorganization, child development, discrimination, disabilities, problems of the poor, unemployment, aging.
15. Knowledge of living conditions and the values of ethnic and subcultural groups, of human growth and behavior, family functioning, child behavior patterns, and environmental factors affecting individuals.
16. Knowledge of modern principles and practices in the specialized phases of social work and of their relationship to current social, psychological and economic problems on an individual and community basis.

TABLE 3.7 (Cont.)

17. Knowledge of food stamp program (agency guidelines, regulations, policies, processes, program effectiveness, results, and statistics).
18. Knowledge of the principles and managerial techniques involved in supervision.
19. Knowledge of the principles and practices of public personnel administration.
20. Knowledge of court procedures relating to guardianship, illegitimacy, and similar situations affecting services to children.
21. Knowledge of child behavior patterns and environmental factors affecting children, and ability to understand and follow proper methods of working with children's cases influenced by these factors and community groups.
22. Skill in the application of interviewing techniques.
23. Ability to recognize conflicting facts that might indicate possible fraud.
24. Ability to use arithmetic to add, subtract, multiply, and divide whole numbers.
25. Ability to carry out instructions in oral and written form.
26. Ability to read and understand complex instructions, such as regulatory policies, and interpret for lay persons.
27. Ability to elicit needs of people from oral discussion.
28. Ability to give simple oral and written instructions.
29. Ability to apply written standards to a variety of observations.
30. Ability to prepare concise case histories.
31. Ability to meet and deal successfully with the public.
32. Ability to assign, direct, and review the work of subordinates.
33. Ability to evaluate effects of administrative procedures.
34. Ability to exercise judgment in evaluating situations and making decisions.
35. Ability to write technical, professional, and administrative reports.
36. Ability to ascertain facts by interviewing individuals, examining records, and making general observations.
37. Ability to establish and maintain effective working relationships with associates, clients, and the public.
38. Ability to communicate clearly and effectively, both orally and in writing.
39. Ability to establish and maintain effective contacts with clients, relatives, and interested individuals and agencies.
40. Ability to use supervision and consultation to increase degree of competency.
41. Ability to exercise judgment and discretion in applying directions of superiors.
42. Ability to meet and deal effectively with superiors, associates, department employees, job applicants, and the general public.
43. Ability to formulate policy and design and install office forms and procedures to meet operating needs.
44. Ability to exercise judgment in planning and initiating a modern program of social work.
45. Ability to train and instruct workers in proper casework methods.
46. Ability to work with and speak before various governmental, civic, and professional organizations.
47. Ability to write or supervise the preparation of professional, technical, operating, and administrative reports and papers.

This framework was developed by the department for use in the study. The 47 statements run the gamut of content as well as specificity. In general, they describe various types of information and skill. Some describe specific content, such as knowledge of forms, agency standards, and local resources. Other statements deal with broader knowledge of federal programs, societal problems, and human processes. The same is true of the skills: some are specific, while others relate to academic and adaptive skills that are basic to the world of work. The configuration is far from ideal, but, despite its obvious flaws, it was considered a useful tool for describing basic worker aptitudes.

Establishing Linkages

The subject matter experts used a three-step scale to make their judgments. For each task, they indicated whether the knowledge or skill (1) was required at the time of employment in order to perform the task adequately; (2) was required in order to perform the task adequately but could be or usually was gained through some form of training after entry; or (3) was not required but, if present, was likely to contribute to superior performance or advancement potential. The raters were not restricted in the number of attributes they could link to a given task. As with the other ratings, they were asked to rate only those tasks with which they were familiar.

The linkage process was based on consensus. A knowledge or skill was linked to a task if at least half of the experts agreed on its scale value as a requirement. At the cluster level, the linkage went through a two-stage process. A knowledge or skill had to be associated with two-thirds of the tasks in a cluster and, for each of these tasks, also had to be identified as needed by 40 percent of the SMEs evaluating the cluster. These criteria were set arbitrarily. In this analysis, emphasis was placed on gaining general impressions rather than on carrying out a rigorous quantitative procedure.

Results

As one might expect, the experts didn't always agree. There was fairly good consensus, however, around a limited set of knowledge and skill requirements. Since the agency was interested in learning more about the needed content of academic and in-service training, we analyzed only the first two scale levels. These data are presented in Tables 3.8 and 3.9, which contain only the attributes that met the

TABLE 3.8
Required Knowledge and Skills for JAS Clusters

Knowledge and Skills

	Linkage	Teaching	Counseling, Informing	Personal Care	Case Management (Specific)	Compiling Information	External Relations	Management of Tangibles	Program Management	Employee Supervision	Case Management (General)	Paper Flow
1			x		x					xx		
2					x							
3	xx		xx		xx							x
5							x	x				
6												
7	x		x									
8			x				x					
9	x		x				x					
12							x		x			
14		x	xx									
15	x	xx	xx							x		
17			xx					x		x	x	
18			xx									
22			xx		x							
23					x				xx	xx		xx
24					xx	xx		xx			xx	xx
25					x	xx		xx			xx	
26					x				xx	xx		
27					x							xx
28		xx	xx			xx						
29				xx			xx				x	
31					xx		xx		x	xx		
32									x	x		
33	x								x	xx		
34					xx	x	x				x	
36					xx		xx			xx	xx	
37	xx	x	xx						xx	xx	x	
38	xx	xx	x		xx		xx		xx	xx		xx
39			x									
40					x		x					
42									x			
43									xx			
44									x	x		
45												
47									x			

Key: xx = required at time of employment; x = required, learn after entry.

61

criteria for inclusion. Table 3.8 contains detailed findings at the cluster level: Table 3.9 summarizes the data for the five job families. Table 3.9 was put together by listing the knowledge and skills that, in a given family, were associated with clusters having Z-scores greater than zero (see the profiles in Figures 3.2 through 3.6). In other words, Table 3.9 contains worker attributes associated only with the activities carried out most frequently by workers in a job family.

Table 3.9 provides a good overview. Most of the entry requirements seem to fall into one of four categories. Clinical knowledge and skills, characterized by such attributes as interviewing skill, knowledge of human development, and awareness of social problems and environmental influences, are concerned primarily with identifying and meeting needs of clients. Organizational skills, such as knowledge of eligibility criteria and the abilities to detect fraud, to formulate policy, and to supervise the work of others, reflect the fact that practice takes place in a public sector bureaucracy, with an ever-present need for accountability. These skills are required for the economic and political viability of the organization. The third set of skills can be called interpersonal attributes. These include such abilities as maintaining working relationships, meeting effectively with the public, eliciting needs from people, and using supervision and consultation effectively. A final group has been characterized as adaptive skills. These include such basic skills as the ability to read and understand instructions, to communicate clearly, and to follow orders. They are the fundamental precursor attributes that are necessary for functioning in the world of work.

Table 3.9 also depicts the required knowledge and skills that could be acquired on the job. In this area there are few surprises. Most of these attributes constitute the content of traditional in-service training or orientation programs, including knowledge of state laws and program requirements, familiarity with current regulations, knowledge of the agency's role, and familiarity with community resources and problems. In short, they are specific to the *site* of practice rather than to the *nature* of practice.

The overall pattern of worker requirements reflects the earlier observation that practice seems to fall into two major divisions, direct and indirect. For example, Table 3.9 shows that there is a good deal of similarity in the requirements for supervisors (family 4) and administrators (family 5). These are the indirect practitioners responsible for making policy, establishing operating procedures, and supervising other workers. The first three families are the direct practitioners. They require the same interpersonal and adaptive skills as the indirect practitioners but have a somewhat greater requirement for clinical

TABLE 3.9
Required Knowledge and Skills for JAS Job Families

	Job Families				
Knowledge and Skills	Para-professionals (1)	Eligibility Workers (2)	Social Service Workers (3)	Supervisors (4)	Admin-istrators (5)
1		x	x	xx	xx
2		x	x		
3	xx	xx	xx		
5		x	x	x	x
6				x	x
7			x		
8	x		x	x	x
9			x	x	
12	x		x	x	x
14	x		xx	x	x
15	xx		xx	x	
17		x	x	x	x
18				x	x
22		x	xx		
23		xx	x		
24		xx	xx	xx	xx
25		xx	xx	xx	xx
26		xx	x	xx	xx
27		x	xx		
28	xx	xx	xx	xx	xx
29		x		x	x
31	xx	xx	xx	xx	xx
32				xx	xx
33		x		x	x
34	x	xx	xx	xx	xx
36		xx	xx	x	x
37	xx		xx	xx	xx
38	xx	xx	xx	xx	xx
39	xx		x		
40		x	x		
42				x	x
43				xx	xx
44				x	x
45				x	x
47				x	x

Key: xx = required at time of employment; x = required, learn after entry.

skills. In general, however, the analysis seems to highlight more similarities than differences in the perceived requirements for workers in the various job families. We attribute this to the strong organizational context characteristic of social work practice in the public sector.

SUMMARY

The overall impression emerging from the analysis of the task data is a sense of order and predictability. The model for practice that emerges, though heterogeneous in method, content, and purpose, can be described succinctly. There are five major streams of practice, each of which is represented by a family of jobs. Personal care is the exclusive domain of the paraprofessionals (family 1). Another group of employees, sizable in number, is responsible for the determination of eligibility (family 2). The social service workers (family 3) come closest to fitting the mold of the traditional social worker, with a clinical thrust. The supervisors (family 4) are responsible mainly for personnel administration and unit management. The final group (family 5) are administrators who carry out the policy implementation and program management tasks of the department. Twenty job groups, varying greatly in size, weave themselves around these major families. Each group represents some specialization by program, activity, or problem.

A number of general characteristics emerge from the analysis. The number of workers who fit the traditional image of the caseworker is small; only 27 percent of the sample are Social Service Workers. However, a relatively large number of workers, 23 percent of the sample, are involved with supervision and administration. The largest single group is the Eligibility Worker family; it constitutes one-third of the sample. In short, it would seem that the nature of public welfare practice is such that it extends far beyond the boundaries of the sterotypical client-centered caseworker.

A number of activities that emerge as clusters are similar to the original SREB roles. Linkage, advocacy, instruction, information processing, administration, and continuing care are cases in point. Thus, the empirical analysis supports a number of the propositions of the early SREB model. There are some differences, however. Practice is usually specialized. The service generalist, as described in the SREB model, is rarely to be found. Also, practice is remedial rather than anticipatory; preventive intervention is seldom mentioned. Large case loads and strict eligibility requirements conspire to make primary prevention a somewhat unlikely endeavor in public welfare. The same seems to be true of advocacy. Little mention is made of activities aggressively directed toward changing the nature of services or of the system itself. These characteristics are probably not unique to this department. The advocate and the generalist, as concepts, both have strong intellectual and emotional appeal—especially to educators. However, they are far easier to conceptualize than to implement in contemporary public agencies. (The implications of these findings and others presented in later chapters are discussed in detail in Chapter 6.)

Additional analyses were carried out with the task data. Subject matter experts rated each task on a number of attributes. These job attributes were combined into a composite index of importance for each job group. When this index was correlated with existing salary schedules in the department, a high positive correlation was obtained.

These same experts also made judgments about the abilities and skills required for job performance. These, too, were pooled into requirements profiles for task clusters and job families. Four major groups of knowledge and abilities surfaced from the ratings by the experts: clinical, organizational, interpersonal, and adaptive. In general, the abilities selected tended to emphasize similarities rather than differences among the jobs and families. The raters concentrated on organizational rather than clinical knowledge and skills. This may be due, in part, to an imbalance in the list used by the raters, but we do see an emphasis being placed on the nonclinical aspects of job requirements.[4]

An image is created that, in this department, social work practice is firmly encased in a bureaucratic container. Depending on the expectations of workers and supervisors, frustrations and dissatisfaction could result from such a situation. This aspect of organizational life can only be explored by closely examining the affective side of the work place. In Chapter 2, it was mentioned that the JAS contains an extensive section dealing with job satisfaction and self-reported reactions to job characteristics. The second half of this book focuses on the relationships between the job content just described and the morale of the workers in the agency.

NOTES

1. These standard scores were based on the frequency data generated in Part I of the JAS. All analyses were carried out at the Seebeck Computer Center of the University of Alabama. Data were processed using a UNIVAC-1100 system and the specialized Program Library developed by Drs. Harry and Barbara Barker of the University of Alabama.

2. Comments have already been made about changes in educational opportunities for minority students in social work programs in the state. Changes are taking place in the employment situation as well.

3. The scales used by the experts to rate these attributes are contained in Appendix F. The scales are based, in part, on the work of Turner and Lawrence (1965).

4. The clinical knowledge and skills contained in the list, in addition to being less numerous, were more diffuse and lacked specificity. Other lists developed for more recent content validation studies, such as the one developed for the Michigan Department of Civil Service (Hatchett 1978), contain more extensive listings of clinical knowledge and abilities.

4

Job Characteristics and Satisfaction: A Model

A CHANGING VIEW OF THE WORLD OF WORK

Taylorism—A Two-Edged Sword

Ever since the early 1920s, when Frederick Taylor convinced American industry to design production jobs accoring to the principles of scientific management, managers have struggled with the mixed blessings of that philosophy. The technological changes it engendered transformed the world of work from a "milieu naturel" into a "milieu technique" (Friedman 1961). In the former condition, characteristic of the preindustrial and craft period, work was organized along skill lines and tradition was a valued criterion for decision making. In the milieu technique, the natural processes of work were intentionally altered by the machine. Scientific management opposed tradition and "laid down the rule that any natural or tradition-guided development was to be viewed with suspicion and that its existence was, in itself, reason enough to change it" (Davis and Taylor 1972, p. 10).

No one will argue that the benefits of this movement were not quick in coming. The standardization of work procedures produced tremendous gains in productivity and efficiency. The next half century saw America become an industrial giant. Recently, however, expert observers are beginning to point to signs of deep malaise in the work place—increased alienation from work and a decline in productivity (Sheppard and Herrick 1971; O'Toole 1973). These are seen as long-term consequences of Taylorism—a crisis in the work place brought about by extensive bureaucratization and by jobs designed more for robots than people (Hackman and Lee 1979). The human services industry has not been without its problems. In the mental health and social service literature, articles documenting the existence of worker "burnout" appear regularly.[1] In his forword to *The Welfare Industry*, Gerald Suttles (1979) has focused on the alienation between workers and clients engendered by the structural characteristics of the public welfare system:

> The whole thrust of the welfare bureaucracy has been toward an industrial processing model with all of its faults when the objects of attention are people rather than lug bolts (p. 11).

The Decline of Industrial Determinism

Periodic shouts of crisis are to be expected in the policy sciences, but the feeling that all is not well in the work place is pervasive. The widespread acceptance of Taylor's imperatives resulted in a deeply rooted technological determinism. For decades, the research carried out by industrial and methods engineers concentrated on a rather simplistic manipulation of physical variables. Machines were designed with little concern for the humans who would operate them. Jobs, when they were studied at all, were viewed as the residue of the engineering process. The work environment was simply the setting for the hardware of production; it was to be made safe whether or not it was pleasant. Much of the time it was neither.

By the late 1920s, methods engineering had become an established tool of industry. The focus was on production. In keeping with this, Western Electric launched an ambitious study at its Hawthorne Works at Cicero, Illinois. It began as a straightforward investigation into the relationship between productivity and the conditions of work. It soon evolved into something very different. Its findings, reported by Mayo (1933) and Roethlisberger and Dickson (1939) have become classic, forever laying to rest the assumption of a neat correspondence between the conditions of work and the productivity of workers.

The findings of this landmark study softened the grip of technology and sparked an interest the social aspects of the work setting and the influences of the work group. Most important, by showing that workers would produce even under the most adverse conditions, the study began to raise questions about the relationship between the nature of work and worker acceptance.

Attention to the Work Itself

The Hawthorne studies triggered an interest in studying the correlates of worker satisfaction. Starting with the early work of Hoppock (1935), research in this area continues unabated to this day. Much of this work has attempted to relate satisfaction to the nature of the work performed by workers. Obviously, such an approach requires measures of the variables in question. Consequently, there was a need to develop a framework for defining and measuring the salient characteristics of work.

Measuring Job Attributes

In 1965 this need was partially met when the first comprehensive work dealing with job attributes was published by Turner and Lawrence. They developed scales for six requisite task attributes (RTAs) that they felt were related to worker satisfaction. They combined the scale values into an index and examined the reactions of workers to jobs with differing RTA values. Finding no clear association between the two variables, except for certain types of workers, they speculated that subcultural characteristics of the workers acted as moderators. The major contribution of the Taylor and Lawrence work was the construction of standardized scales for the measurement presumed to be present in all jobs. Much of the subsequent work done with job attributes has been patterned after their approach.[2]

Redesigning Work

As stated earlier, many experts believe that the composition of most modern industrial jobs leaves much to be desired. Unlike their predecessors, however, contemporary theorists no longer tend to think of jobs as static, unchangeable entities. In fact, there has been an active advocacy of the process of job redesign. The intentional manipulation of job characteristics is usually seen as a way of bringing about desired employee responses (increased production and satisfaction) or reducing undesired responses (boredom, alienation, turnover). Several theories provide the impetus behind the job redesign movement in industry. They are reviewed by Hackman and Lee (1979) and need not be recounted here. Basically, they all posit a relationship between attributes of the job and affective responses of workers. These affective states are then assumed to be linked to various job behaviors (productivity, turnover, absenteeism). One of these theories shaped the collection of data in the present study.

Job Attributes and the DPS Study

As has been demonstrated in the first half of this book, the job-centered portion of the Job Analysis Survey captures the specific task content of the work performed by various employees in the Alabama Department of Pensions and Security (DPS). By so doing, it permits one to make fine differentiations among the various patterns of work in the department. The second half of the questionnaire, not yet discussed, has a different purpose. It is designed to characterize the jobs in the department in terms of a limited set of job attributes. In addition, it provides a vehicle for the workers to react to their jobs and to various aspects of the work setting.

We included data about job attributes and satisfaction in the study for several reasons. First, it had been a long time since a systematic attitude survey had been carried out in the department. Consequently, little was known about employee reactions to jobs and working conditions. Second, the belief existed that some job modifications might be in order. If worker responses to various job attributes were known, such knowledge might be of use in planning the alterations. Finally, we believed that the DPS study, which would produce detailed job information, would be an ideal vehicle to carry out some related research on the job satisfaction of social workers.

Any approach to data collection has to stem, at least implicitly, from some theoretical point of view. The present study was no exception. In formulating the methodology, we drew heavily from the work of Hackman and Oldham. Since it forms the basis for a significant portion of the data collection effort, some time will be devoted to its description.

THE JOB DIAGNOSTIC SURVEY

Basic Rationale

Most theorists would agree that the assumption of a linear relationship between job characteristics and employee reactions is a naive one. The early work of Turner and Lawrence (1965) suggested the presence of moderators, and subsequent work by Blood and Hulin (1967) reinforced it. Recent contributions to the literature caution against simplistic views of this domain.[3] Theorists believe that some type of contingency theory is the safest theoretical perspective to work from. In other words, employees will react negatively or positively to their jobs, but their responses will be moderated by a variety of situational variables.

This is the position taken by Hackman and his colleagues. Korman, Greenhaus, and Badin (1977) sum up their approach nicely:

> to develop and validate an instrument, the Job Diagnostic Survey (JDS), which attempts to tap the motivating potential of a job, the current level of employee satisfaction and motivation, and the level of employees' "growth needs" or the readiness to perform on an enriched job (p. 186).

These various components were formulated into a job characteristics model of work motivation. An illustration of the model is presented in Figure 4.1. The model suggest that positive personal and work outcomes are obtained when three critical psychological states exist in a job incumbent. These states are brought about in response to five core job dimensions. Jobs that are high in skill variety, task identity, and task significance are seen to produce a high level of meaningfulness of work. Jobs that are high in autonomy result in increased feelings of responsibility. Increased knowledge of result can be expected from jobs that provide a good deal of feedback. The model does not assume a direct relationship among the three sets of variables. In fact, Hackman and Oldham (1975) have stated:

> People who strongly value and desire personal feelings of accomplishment and growth should respond very positively to a job which is high

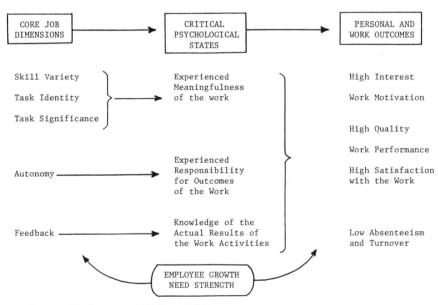

Source: Hackman and Oldham 1974*a*.

FIGURE 4.1. The Job Characteristics Model of Work Motivation

on the core dimensions; individuals who do not value personal growth and accomplishment may find such a job anxiety arousing and may be uncomfortably "stretched" by it (p. 160).

In line with this thinking, they postulated that a variable called "growth-need strength" serves as a moderator of the various relationships specified in the model.

Measuring the Components of the Model

To test the theory, Hackman and Oldham have devised a self-report questionnaire called the Job Diagnostic Survey (JDS).[4] The instrument contains items that measure various components of the model. Long and short versions of the JDS have been developed. The short form of the instrument was used in the present study because the other data requirements were so extensive. In using the short form, we assumed that there might be a loss in scale reliability, but to use the long form would have unduly burdened the respondents and might have jeopardized the main thrust of the study. The items used in the short form can be found in Appendix C. The last section of the JAS questionnaire (Part III) contains the short form of the JDS. With the exception of Part III-D, responses are measured on a seven-point scale (1 = low, 7 = high). Reverse scoring is used with some items to construct the various scales.

Job Dimensions

The core job dimensions are measured by the 14 items in Part III-A of the questionnaire. The dimensions and the items measuring them are as follows:

Skill Variety: The degree to which a job requires the worker to engage in different activities involving a number of different skills. *Items 1 and 5 (reversed).*

Task Identity: The degree to which the job requires the completion of work that can be identified as a whole entity. *Items 11 and 3 (reversed).*

Task Significance: The degree to which the job has an impact on the lives of others—inside or outside the job environment. *Items 8 and 14 (reversed).*

Autonomy: The degree to which the schedules and procedures on the job permit the worker to exercise independent judgment and discretion. *Items 13 and 9 (reversed).*

Feedback from the Job Itself: The degree to which the work activities convey clear information about how well or poorly the worker performs. *Items 4 and 12 (reversed).*

The JDS contains items measuring two supplemental dimensions not explicitly called for in the model:

Feedback from Agents: The degree to which supervisors or other workers provide information about the quality of the worker's performance. *Items 10 and 7 (reversed).*

Dealing with Others: The degree to which the job activity requires the worker to interact and work closely with people—either co-workers or clients. *Items 2 and 6 (reversed).*

Psychological States

As the model depicts, three psychological states are assumed to be brought about in response to the attributes of the job. As the short form of the JDS does not contain items relating to these variables, we did not collect them as part of the study.

Personal and Work Outcomes

Some of the outcomes described in the model, such as performance, absenteeism, and turnover, cannot be assessed by means of a self-report questionnaire. Others, however, are more amenable to this type of format and are included in the JDS. These items are found in Part III-B of the survey booklet. The affective states covered by them are as follows:

General Satisfaction: The extent to which the worker is satisfied or happy with the overall nature of the job. *Items 2, 6, and 4 (reversed).*

Internal Work Motivation: The degree to which the motivation to work comes from *within* the worker. The items try to assess the extent to which the worker experiences positive or negative feelings when doing well or poorly on the job. *Items 1, 3, 5, and 7 (reversed).*

Part III-C contains items measuring specific sources of satisfaction. They include Pay (Items 2 and 9), Job Security (Items 1 and 11), Social Interactions (Items 4, 7, and 12), Supervision (Items 5, 8, and 14), and Opportunity for Growth (Items 3, 6, 10, and 13).

Growth-Need Strength

The 12 items in Part III-D tap the important variable of growth need. This construct is viewed as the moderator that influences how positively a worker will respond to a job with a high motivating potential. In the original JDS short form, this variable was measured by having people indicate the degree to which they would like to have jobs with certain specific characteristics. In reviewing the instrument, we were concerned about distortion in responses because of the obvious social desirability of some of the items. (Hackman and Oldham caution about the possibility of faking responses to the JDS, which is a problem with most instruments of this kind.) As a result, the alternate version of this measure was used. It resembles a forced-choice format in that the respondent must choose, in each item, between a pair of jobs with different characteristics. One of the jobs in each pair has characteristics relevant to growth-need satisfaction, the other is related to a different type of satisfaction. The respondent indicates a preference for one or the other by using a five-point scale. The growth need of a respondent is the average of his ratings for the 12 items. Half the items use reverse scoring.

Motivating Potential Score

A summary measure, called the motivating potential score (MPS), can be generated from responses to the various scales in the JDS. The formula is as follows:

$$MPS = \left[\frac{\text{Skill Variety} + \text{Task Identity} + \text{Task Significance}}{3} \right] \times \left[\text{Autonomy} \right] \times \left[\text{Feedback from Job} \right]$$

Within the context of the theory, the MPS value represents the inherent potential of the job to motivate the employee. The worker presumably responds to the core characteristics contained in this index—a response strongly influenced by the level of his or her personal need for growth.

Psychometric Properties of the Instrument

Reliability of the Scales

As mentioned earlier, some loss in reliability was expected in using the short form of the JDS. To confirm this and to assess the adequacy of the data, we computed internal consistency reliabilities of the various scales, as summarized in Table 4.1. Also presented are the reliabilities obtained by Hackman and Oldham as part of the standardization of the long form of the JDS. Both sets of coefficients were computed in basically the same fashion; they can therefore be compared to each other directly. As expected, the present study's reliability coefficients are generally lower than those obtained by use of the long form. Of all the scales, the satisfaction data are the most reliable. Some of the job dimension scales, Task Significance, and Feedback from the Job Itself, have very low coefficients. However, given the significant time savings with the use of the short form, the reliability loss is acceptable. We might wish for higher reliabilities but, as Hackman and Oldham (1975) stated, "the intent was to develop scales composed of items with heterogeneous content—to maximize the substantive 'richness' of each measure" (p. 169).

TABLE 4.1
Reliabilities of the JDS Scales

JDS Scale	Internal Consistency Reliability	
	Present Study[a]	Published Data[b]
Job Dimensions		
Skill Variety	.61	.71
Task Identity	.73	.59
Task Significance	.23	.66
Autonomy	.58	.66
Feedback from the Job Itself	.43	.71
Feedback from Agents	.62	.78
Dealing with Others	.41	.59
Affective Responses		
Internal Work Motivation	.53	.76
General Satisfaction	.72	.76
Specific Satisfactions:		
Job Security	.62	—[c]
Pay	.89	—[c]
Social Interactions	.64	.56
Supervision	.86	.79
Growth	.81	.84
Growth-Need Strength		
Job Choice Format	.72	.71

[a]Reliability was computed by obtaining the mean interitem correlation for the items scored on each scale and then adjusting that value by means of the Spearman-Brown procedure.

[b]Data taken from Hackman and Oldham (1975), based on complete JDS instrument using a sample of 658 respondents.

[c]Data not available since these were new scales at the time initial standardization data were published.

Relationships among the Scales

Intercorrelations among the various JDS scales are presented in Table 4.2. In general, they conform to the patterns described in Hackman and Oldham's original standardization material. For the most part, the correlations among the various job dimensions are moderately positively correlated; the average intercorrelation is .16. Since the job dimensions are expressed in positive language, this is not unexpected. Jobs, when they are "good," tend to be good in a number of ways. Often the converse is also true.

The model would suggest that job attributes should be positively correlated with satisfaction. To a certain extent, the data support this. The average intercorrelation between the two clusters of variables is .18. The moderator variable, Growth-Need Strength, also behaves as expected. With an average intercorrelation of .05 with the other variables, it is independent of the various components of the model. It would thus seem, at least in terms of the discriminant validity of the various scales, that the model is behaving as it should.

Mean Scale Values

In order to complete the psychometric characterization of the instrument, we calculated the mean and variance for each of the scales. The pattern of means for the DPS sample is presented in Table 4.3, along with those obtained from several published studies using the JDS. The Hackman and Oldham data are based on the original standardization sample, which consisted of 658 workers in 62 different jobs. Scattered in seven different organizations, the jobs vary from blue-collar to professional. Some service organizations are included in the sample, but all were drawn from the private sector. In contrast, the data from Van Maanan and Katz are from the public sector. All the workers were employed in either state, county, or city government. The original Van Maanan sample included more than 3,000 workers. For comparison purposes, a subset of 1,736 workers was extracted from it. This sample includes only those workers who are most comparable to the DPS group, including administrators, professionals, technicians, protective service workers, and paraprofessionals. These jobs are not restricted to social service positions but include a variety of medical, legal, and technical activities as well.

An inspection of Table 4.3 reveals a number of interesting features. First, the pattern of means for the DPS sample reflects wide differences from scale to scale. Such variability is encouraging, since

TABLE 4.2
Matrix of Intercorrelations among JDS Scales

	Skill Variety	Task Identity	Task Significance	Autonomy	Feedback: Job	Feedback: Agents	Dealing with Others	Internal Work Motivation	General Satisfaction	Job Security	Pay	Social Interaction	Supervision	Growth	Growth-Need Strength
Skill Variety		-.10	.35	.20	.25	.14	.37	.20	.24	.12	-.02	.11	.05	.35	.15
Task Identity			-.01	.15	.12	.11	-.08	.07	.19	.05	.10	.06	.08	.05	.02
Task Significance				.16	.23	.11	.32	.21	.21	.11	.05	.16	.10	.24	.08
Autonomy					.24	.11	.13	.19	.30	.23	.13	.30	.13	.47	.08
Feedback—Job						.24	.15	.28	.34	.15	.06	.16	.18	.33	.08
Feedback—Agents							.12	.17	.27	.12	.03	.20	.52	.22	-.02
Dealing with Others								.07	.06	.08	.02	.01	.02	.13	.05
Internal Work Motivation									.52	.14	.17	.34	.20	.47	-.01
General Satisfaction										.20	.19	.42	.36	.58	.00
Job Security											.35	.18	.24	.32	-.06
Pay												.15	.18	.24	-.04
Social Interaction													.34	.64	-.05
Supervision														.37	-.04
Growth															-.05
Growth-Need Strength															

Note: Numbers are Pearson product-moment correlations (r). Correlations greater than ±.08 are significantly different from zero ($p < .05$).

77

TABLE 4.3
Comparison of Mean JDS Job Dimensions with Other Samples

JDS Scales	Present Study[a]	Hackman and Oldham[b]	Van Maanan and Katz[c]	Critical Ratio[d] (Significance)
Job Dimensions				
Skill Variety	5.54	4.49	5.68	12.29**
Task Identity	4.72	4.87	5.14	1.67†
Task Significance	6.28	5.49	6.11	11.58**
Autonomy	5.34	4.80	5.29	7.07**
Feedback from the Job Itself	5.02	4.98	5.17	.53†
Feedback from Agents	5.05	3.98	4.18	11.95**
Dealing with Others	6.35	5.29	6.03	16.50**
Affective Responses				
Internal Work Motivation	5.95	5.39	5.77	11.91**
General Satisfaction	5.62	4.62	—[e]	17.08**
Specific Satisfactions:				
Job Security	5.55	—[e]	—[e]	—
Pay	4.71	—[e]	—[e]	—
Social Interactions	5.82	5.42	—[e]	8.51**
Supervision	5.42	5.28	—[e]	1.95†
Growth	5.31	4.82	—[e]	7.37**
Growth-Need Strength				
Job Choice Format	3.24	—[e]	—[e]	—

[a]Based on the entire sample of 661 public welfare department employees.

[b]Based on a sample of 658 employees in seven organizations (Hackman and Oldham 1975). The JDS long form was used.

[c]Based on a sample of 1,736 employees in state and local government. (Van Maanan, Katz, and Gregg 1974). The JDS long form was used.

[d]Comparisons are based only on the present study and the Hackman and Oldham data.

[e]Data on these scales are not available.

** = $p < .01$.

† = not significant.

it suggests that the instrument is sensitive to sources of variance within the sample. Further inspection of the table shows that, in almost every instance, the mean scale values reported by the private sector workers in the Hackman and Oldham sample are lower than those of the DPS workers in the present study. Tests of the significance of these differences indicate that they should not be attributed to chance. Either the norms of these two groups are indeed different, or a systematic bias has been introduced by virtue of using the short form of the JDS. The Van Maanan, Katz, and Gregg data can be used to shed some light on the possibility of bias. Their study was conducted in the public sector (as was the present study), and the data were collected using the long form of the JDS. Despite this methodological difference, the mean scale values are consistently higher than those from the Hackman and Oldham sample and, in most instances, are extremely close to the DPS sample values. (The original Van Maanan, Katz, and Gregg data were not available to us, so differences between them and the DPS data could not be tested. Assuming similar standard errors, however, most of the differences would not be statistically significant.) These data suggest that the findings from the present study may well be typical of the public sector and that the short form of the JDS has not introduced any major artifacts into the research. In short, the results of the preliminary analyses suggest that the instrument is satisfactory and that further research on the model can proceed.

Rationale for Subsequent Analyses

As is now evident, a wide range of data was collected in the present study. For each of the 661 DPS workers in the sample we obtained information about job activity (at the task, cluster, job group, and job family level), job discretion, perceived job attributes, general and specific sources of job satisfaction, and growth needs. In addition to this array of job-related data, key elements of personal history (biodata) were also obtained. As such, this data base constitutes a rich pool of research material.

More specifically, these data provide an excellent opportunity for (1) evaluating how well the Hackman and Oldham model (job characteristics theory) seems to fit in a public sector social services job setting; (2) relating job attributes obtained from the JDS format to job characteristics derived from the JAS and from ratings of subject matter experts; and (3) examining the nature of growth-need strength by relating it to a number of personal history variables.

The next chapter will describe the research steps implied by the foregoing exposition, present the data generated by them, and interpret the findings.

NOTES

1. An excellent review of this material can be found in Pines and Kafrey (1978) and Pines and Maslach (1978).

2. See, for example, the work of Hackman and Lawler (1971); Hackman and Oldham (1974a, 1974b, 1975); Jenkins et al. (1975); Dunham (1976, 1977); Sims, Szilagyi, and Keller (1976).

3. See, for example, Korman, Greenhaus, and Badin (1977).

4. The JDS has undergone extensive testing and revision. For more detail concerning its makeup and standardization, consult the materials by Hackman and his collaborators (Hackman and Lawler 1971; Hackman and Oldham 1974a, 1974b, 1975).

5

Job Attributes and Satisfaction: Findings

THE VALIDITY OF THE JOB DIAGNOSTIC SURVEY

Having satisfactorily established that the short form of the JDS was a reasonably reliable instrument, our next step was to investigate its validity. Our logic was fairly simple. It seemed reasonable to assume that the groupings formed in the JAS analyses should differ not only in task content but also in terms of the more abstract job properties supposedly tapped by the JDS. If this were so, differences in the JDS scale values would also be found among the various job groups. Since the JAS groups were formed without reference to the JDS variables, one part of the data could thus serve as a check, that is, a concurrent validation criterion, for the other.

Discrimination among the JAS Groupings

An analysis of the JDS means was carried out. Our first step was to look at the values of the core job dimensions for the groups formed in the analysis of the JAS data. These values can be found in Table 5.1. At first, the table may be confusing, but it does indicate that the job groups and families vary greatly on the JDS dimensions. To test the statistical significance of these apparent differences, we carried out multiple comparisons for all possible pairs of means. To strengthen the reliability of the comparisons, we used only the means of the five job families.

Since there are eight JDS scales, 80 such comparisions are possible. Of these, 47 are significantly different from one another. (A cut-off point of $p < .05$ was set on an a priori basis. At this level, only four

TABLE 5.1
Mean Values on the Core Job Dimensions for the JAS Job Groups

JAS Group[a]	Skill Variety	Task Identity	Task Significance	Autonomy	Feedback: Job	Feedback: Agents	Dealing With Others	Motivating Potential Score
				JDS Core Job Dimensions				
1	4.00	4.90	5.50	5.23	4.23	5.00	5.07	106.87
2	3.04	5.26	5.37	5.68	4.56	5.04	5.61	123.92
Family 1	3.49	5.16	5.42	5.44	4.47	5.02	5.42	118.11
5	5.16	5.09	6.16	4.98	4.76	4.60	5.90	135.01
8	4.85	5.16	6.28	4.57	4.99	5.09	5.99	130.03
9	5.06	4.96	6.25	4.96	4.89	4.58	6.20	138.14
10	5.44	4.79	6.47	5.23	5.09	5.18	6.31	154.80
11	5.64	5.33	6.34	5.45	5.03	4.83	6.43	168.09
Family 2	5.20	5.03	6.30	5.01	4.95	4.85	6.16	143.75
6	5.88	4.40	6.20	5.34	4.72	4.97	6.29	140.83
7	5.80	4.73	5.97	5.70	4.90	5.62	6.51	155.79
12	5.64	5.42	6.47	6.17	5.42	5.44	6.30	198.89
13	5.80	4.94	6.11	5.50	4.83	4.92	6.48	155.36
Family 3	5.81	4.73	6.15	5.56	4.87	5.17	6.40	154.31
14	6.01	4.66	6.50	5.41	5.38	5.28	6.84	171.82
17	5.42	4.89	6.32	4.82	5.66	5.16	6.53	154.74
19	5.88	4.70	6.62	6.02	5.54	5.18	6.52	195.07
Family 4	5.84	4.73	6.49	5.46	5.49	5.23	6.67	174.88
15	6.23	3.76	6.58	5.50	5.03	5.04	6.58	161.86
16	6.72	3.86	6.71	5.48	5.60	4.91	6.96	182.81
20	6.45	3.93	6.61	5.84	5.16	4.93	6.75	175.61
Family 5	6.46	3.84	6.63	5.58	5.27	4.96	6.76	172.96

[a]As in our earlier analyses, groups 3, 4, and 18 are not included. Groups 3 and 4 were considered too small, and group 18 was considered too diverse to be interpreted with any clarity.

significant differences could be expected to occur by chance.) The pattern of significance levels is presented in Table 5.2. Taken as a whole, the data clearly indicate that the five JAS families differ considerably on the core dimensions measured by the JDS. The families are most different in the range of skills required (Skill Variety) as well as in the extent to which workers are required to interact and work closely with people (Dealing with Others). At the other extreme, there seem to be no significant differences in the extent to which in-

Table 5.2
Pattern of Significance Levels among the Five JAS Job Families

Skill Variety

	1	2	3	4	5
1		**	**	**	**
2			**	**	**
3				†	**
4					**
5					

Task Identity

	1	2	3	4	5
1		†	†	†	**
2			†	†	**
3				†	**
4					**
5					

Task Significance

	1	2	3	4	5
1		**	*	**	**
2			†	†	**
3				**	**
4					†
5					

Autonomy

	1	2	3	4	5
1		*	†	†	†
2			**	**	**
3				†	†
4					†
5					

Feedback: Job Itself

	1	2	3	4	5
1		*	†	**	**
2			†	**	†
3				**	*
4					†
5					

Feedback: Agents

	1	2	3	4	5
1		†	†	†	†
2			†	†	†
3				†	†
4					†
5					

Dealing with Others

	1	2	3	4	5
1		*	**	**	**
2			**	**	**
3				**	**
4					†
5					

Motivating Potential Score

	1	2	3	4	5
1		*	**	**	**
2			†	**	**
3				*	*
4					†
5					

Note: Numbers refer to job families.

* = $p < .05$

** = $p < .01$

† = not significant

cumbents receive feedback from co-workers or supervisors about their performance (Feedback from Agents). On the other five JDS scales, the results are more mixed. However, they all demonstrate some sensitivity to differences among the job families. In general, values on the JDS scales tend to increase as one moves from the paraprofessionals (family 1) to the administrators (family 5).

The Motivating Potential Score

A central component of the Hackman and Oldham formulation is the notion that the eight job dimensions we have just analyzed determine a job's potential to convey a sense of meaningfulness and responsibility to an incumbent. To reflect this capacity, they devised the motivating potential score (MPS) as a summary measure.[1] We computed an MPS value for each job group and family. These appear in the last colum of Table 5.1. As can be seen, there is considerable variation across the job groups. Again, the familiar pattern of systematic increases from family 1 through family 5 is evident. As before, tests on contrasts were carried out. The results are shown in Table 5.2. Almost all differences among the families are statistically significant. In other words, there seems to be considerable difference in the motivating potential of the jobs. Since the MPS is constructed from the various core components, this finding was not surprising.

Thus far, the results are encouraging. The JDS components seem to interact in ways that are consistent with the proposed framework. In addition to verifying the consistency of the components, however, we thought it important to carry out some additional validity checks. These checks focused on the ratings of the 18 subject matter experts who evaluated the 77 JAS tasks. They rated each task in terms of its criticality, implied discretion, probability of error, and clarity of remedy. As discussed earlier, we combined these ratings into a composite importance index and generated a value for each job group and family.[2] If the MPS truly reflects the meaningfulness and responsibility inherent in a job, it should have a high positive correlation with this importance index. There are two reasons why such a finding would enhance the presumption of validity. First, the ratings on which the importance index is based and the JDS scale values on which the MPS is based were generated by different groups of respondents working independently of one another. Second, the ratings were made at the task level, while the JDS values were collected at the job level. Thus, no contamination between the two measures is very likely and they should be independent estimates of the same basic construct. A correlation was computed between the two variables, and a Pearson coefficient of .83 was obtained. Again, this is an encouraging result.

As a final check, we examined the relationship between the measures of Autonomy and Discretion. The former is a scale in the JDS; the latter is one of the job attributes rated by the subject matter experts. Our rationale was essentially the same as in the previous analysis. Given their definitions, they should be positively correlated. Since they came from independent data sources, high agreement would reflect well on the JDS as an instrument. Again, we computed a correlation between the two measures and, as before, a high Pearson coefficient (r = .80) was obtained. In short, the validity data looked good.

THE SATISFACTION DATA: A TEST OF THE MODEL

Once we had carried out these preliminary tests, we thought it proper to turn our attention to the satisfaction data and the other aspects of the model. As described earlier, the JDS contains six basic satisfaction measures. The first of these—General Satisfaction—is simply a measure of the extent to which a worker feels positively or negatively about his overall job situation. In addition, five specific satisfaction measures are obtained, dealing with pay, job security, social interactions, the quality of supervision, and the extent to which the job provides opportunities for personal growth.

Job Grouping and Satisfaction

Our initial steps in analyzing the satisfaction data were basically the same as those used with the other parts of the JDS. We were first interested in seeing whether workers in the various job groups expressed differing amounts of satisfaction. Data from this analysis can be found in Table 5.3. The results of significance tests are shown in Table 5.4. As with the job dimensions, there is much variation from one JAS group to another. But this time it is not systematic. There is no orderly progression in scores as one moves from the paraprofessionals (family 1) to the administrators (family 5).

It is not easy to pick out patterns from an array of numbers, so we have prepared graphs of the satisfaction values for the five families (see Figures 5.1 through 5.6). A number of things become obvious from these graphs. First, as we have just said, the clear progression of

TABLE 5.3

Mean Values on the JDS Satisfaction Measures for the JAS Job Groups

JAS Group[a]	General Satis-faction	Pay	Job Security	Social	Super-vision	Opportunity for Growth
			JDS Satisfaction Measures			
1	6.38	5.50	5.70	6.71	6.46	6.15
2	5.79	4.63	5.24	6.52	5.89	5.68
Family 1	6.00	4.94	5.40	6.59	6.09	5.85
5	5.48	4.35	5.14	5.58	5.34	4.66
8	5.50	4.84	5.44	5.58	5.72	4.99
9	5.56	4.33	5.60	5.48	5.10	4.71
10	5.55	4.34	5.22	5.81	5.13	5.06
11	5.69	4.86	5.53	5.47	5.14	4.89
Family 2	5.55	4.51	5.39	5.55	5.28	4.86
6	5.39	4.76	5.40	5.77	5.16	5.21
7	5.62	4.94	5.71	5.90	5.64	5.48
12	5.41	4.11	5.36	6.07	5.55	5.50
13	5.50	4.41	5.41	5.81	4.99	5.22
Family 3	5.48	4.65	5.48	5.84	5.28	5.31
14	5.68	5.20	5.72	5.89	5.46	5.56
17	5.60	4.68	6.00	5.56	5.60	5.29
19	5.79	4.74	5.94	5.81	5.84	5.88
Family 4	5.69	4.94	5.85	5.79	5.60	5.59
15	5.80	5.26	5.69	5.98	5.28	5.63
16	5.84	4.41	5.83	6.09	5.36	5.99
20	5.98	5.11	5.75	6.24	5.79	5.91
Family 5	5.87	5.02	5.54	6.09	5.46	5.80

[a]As earlier, groups 3, 4, and 18 are not included in the analyses.

TABLE 5.4

Significance Levels of the Satisfaction Measures for the Five JAS Job Families

	1	2	3	4	5			1	2	3	4	5
	General Satisfaction							*Pay*				
1		**	**	†	†		1		†	†	†	†
2			†	†	**		2			†	*	*
3				†	**		3				†	†
4					†		4					†
5							5					

TABLE 5.4 Continued

Job Security

	1	2	3	4	5
1		†	†	*	†
2			†	**	†
3				**	†
4					*
5					

Social

	1	2	3	4	5
1		**	**	**	**
2			**	*	**
3				†	*
4					*
5					

Supervision

	1	2	3	4	5
1		**	**	**	**
2			†	*	†
3				*	†
4					†
5					

Opportunity for Growth

	1	2	3	4	5
1		**	**	†	†
2			**	**	**
3				*	**
4					†
5					

Note: Numbers refer to job families.

* = $p < .05$

** = $p < .01$

† = not significant

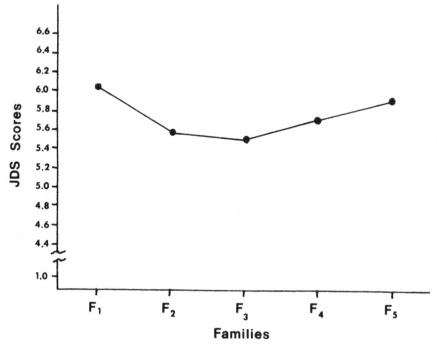

FIGURE 5.1. Satisfaction Means for JAS Job Families: General Satisfaction

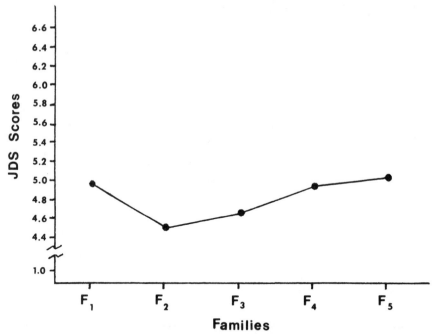

FIGURE 5.2. Satisfaction Means for JAS Job Families: Pay

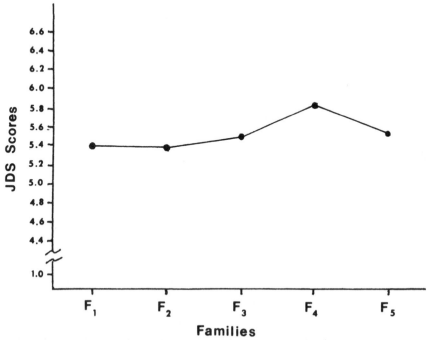

FIGURE 5.3. Satisfaction Means for JAS Job Families: Job Security

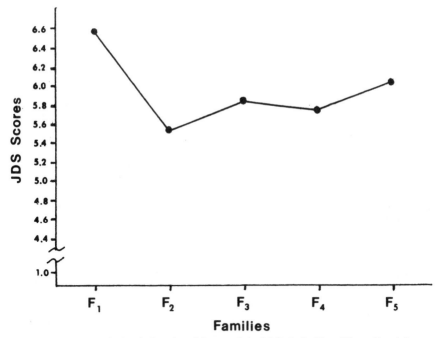

FIGURE 5.4. Satisfaction Means for JAS Job Families: Social

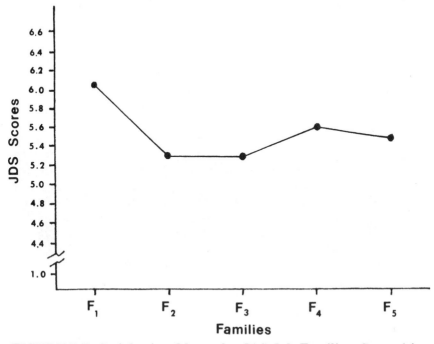

FIGURE 5.5. Satisfaction Means for JAS Job Families: Supervision

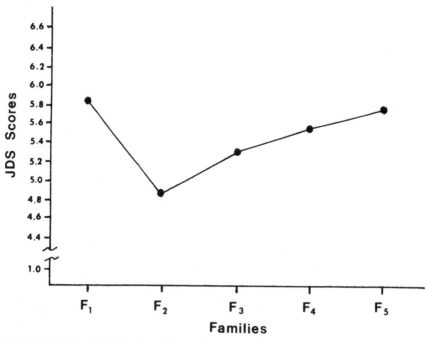

FIGURE 5.6. Satisfaction Means for JAS Job Families: Opportunities
for Growth

scale values is absent. Second, although satisfaction with specific job
features is good, the employees are not very pleased with salaries.
(This finding further attests to the sensitivity of the instrument. At
the time of testing, workers in this agency had lower salaries than
those of their professional counterparts in other state agencies. Since
this had been mentioned by the workers on many occasions, we attribute some of the dissatisfaction to that wage differential.) Finally,
the employees in family 2 (Eligibility Workers) and family 3 (Social
Service Workers) seem to be less satisfied with almost all aspects of
their jobs than do the other workers. This is especially true of the
Eligibility Workers. We believe there are several explanations for this
data pattern. All explanations would involve the introduction of
variables external to the JDS instrument, so rather than interrupt the
flow of discussion, we will discuss them in the next chapter.

The Job as a Motivator

In the introductory section of Chapter 4, we indicated that some
job design theorists have operated on the premise of a strong relation-

ship between job characteristics and affective responses, such as job satisfaction, of workers. In the Hackman and Oldham model, the motivating potential score (MPS) purportedly synthesizes the intrinsic motivational capacity of a particular job. To assess this assumption, we calculated the correlations between this index and the six JDS measures of satisfaction. We also correlated the MPS data with the measure of internal work motivation (IWM). As we saw in Figure 4.1, the satisfaction and work motivation variables are both viewed as work outcomes by Hackman and his colleagues.

The results of these analyses are summarized in Table 5.5. As can be seen, there is clearly a relationship between the MPS variable and the various work outcomes. Although most of the correlations are significant ($p < .05$), the pattern of correlations is somewhat erratic across the five job families. For the total sample ($N = 661$), the highest coefficient is .50. This means that, at best, the MPS can account for only 25 percent of the variance in one of the satisfaction measures. Obviously, some other influences are at work.

The Role of Growth-Need Strength

Hackman and Oldham would neither be surprised nor chagrined by our findings. After all, theirs is a contingency model. They would not expect a simple direct relationship between job characteristics and satisfaction. They contend that workers' reactions to the characteristics of their jobs are moderated by their readiness to perform in an enriched situation. Their formulation maintains that workers would

TABLE 5.5
Correlations between the Motivating Potential Score Job Satisfaction and Internal Work Motivation

| Job Family | *JDS Satisfaction Measures* | | | | | | Internal Work Motivation |
	General Satis- faction	Pay	Job Security	Social	Super- vision	Oppor- tunity for Growth	
1	.10	-.03	-.02	.11	-.12	.00	.19
2	.43	.17	.23	.32	.14	.57	.38
3	.43	.13	.26	.28	.29	.51	.25
4	.57	.22	.29	.28	.29	.51	.26
5	.38	.00	.16	.41	.36	.52	.14
Total Sample	.42	.14	.24	.26	.21	.50	.30

Note: Numbers are Pearson product-moment correlations. For the total sample, values greater than ±.08 are significantly different from zero ($p < .05$).

respond most positively to jobs with motivating potentials that are consistent with the incumbents' need for challenge and growth. In short, high satisfaction should occur when there is a match between two key variables—the motivating potential score of a job and the growth need strength (GNS) of the worker who holds that job. Conversely, low satisfaction should accompany a mismatch between these two variables.

The data permitted us to test this proposition directly. First, we calculated the median MPS value and split the sample in half. We repeated this procedure using the GNS measure. By so doing, we partitioned the sample into four groups. The first group consisted of workers who were above the median in growth-need strength and were also working in jobs with high motivating potential scores that is, above the median. (For the total sample, the median MPS value was 146.25. The upper limit of this variable is 343. The median GNS value was 3.17, based on a five-point scale. The distributions of both these variables were basically symmetrical.) The second group was comprised of workers whose growth-need strength was below the median of the sample and who were in jobs with low motivating potential in that their jobs had MPS values below the median of the sample. According to the model, these two groups should report high job satisfaction because they are matched with jobs suited to their needs for growth and accomplishment. The remaining two groups represent the reverse situation; they are in jobs with motivating potentials opposite to their growth needs. For these two mismatched groups, the model would predict lower satisfaction, since these workers would be either uncomfortably taxed by their jobs or underutilized in them.

In almost all the previous analyses, there have been consistent differences among the various job families. Consequently, we decided to carry out separate analyses for each family in addition to the one based on the entire sample. In this series of analyses, we treated the six satisfaction measures and the internal work motivation measures as if they were dependent variables; that is, we assumed they would vary systematically as a consequence of the match or mismatch between the MPS and GNS variables. Family by family, we calculated the means of the seven dependent variables for each of the four sample groups. (All the dependent variables are measured with a seven-point scale.) These data can be found in Appendixes G and H.

An inspection of these 42 contingency tables seems to suggest support for the Hackman and Oldham thesis. Using multiple comparisons, we ran significance tests on the means of the matched groups and those of mismatched groups. The results of these analyses, presented in Table 5.6 bear out our first impressions. Thirteen of the patterns behave in a manner consistent with the Hackman and Oldham

TABLE 5.6

Results of Contrasts on Work Outcome Measures for Matched and "Mismatched" Workers

Work Outcomes	Family 1 (N = 46)	Family 2 (N = 219)	Family 3 (N = 176)	Family 4 (N = 84)	Family 5 (N= 90)	Entire Sample (N = 661)[a]
General Satisfaction	†	†	†	†	†	*
Pay	†	†	†	†	†	†
Job Security	†	†	†	†	†	*
Social	†	†	†	†	**	**
Supervision	†	†	**	†	**	**
Opportunity for Growth	†	†	†	**	**	**
Internal Work Motivation	†	**	†	*	†	*

[a]The total for the entire sample exceeds that of the sum of the separate families because job groups 3, 4, and 18 were deleted from previous analyses of the family data.

 * = p < .05

** = p < .01

 † = not significant

formulation. To be sure, the results are not overwhelming, but they far exceed what we would have expected to occur by chance. When large numbers of workers are used, as in the analysis based on the entire sample, the pattern is consistent. There does seem to be a decided tendency for the growth-need variable to influence how these workers react to their jobs.

Further Examination of Growth-Need Strength

Because of its role in moderating the affective responses to jobs, we were interested in learning more about the growth-need strength variable, so we carried out some additional analyses. It was obvious from the intercorrelation data (see Table 4.2) that the variable has little direct relationship with either the core job dimensions or the work outcomes. Given its definition, we decided to examine its relationship to various demographic characteristics of the workers.

The first variable we looked at was age. We took the age range of the sample (54 years) and split it into 11 five-year intervals. Using GNS as the dependent variable, we ran a one-way analysis of variance (ANOVA). The analysis indicates that the need to function in enriched jobs does not change significantly with age. It is a different story, however, with formal education. Using eight levels of education, the ANOVA shows a distinct pattern. With these workers, as one moves from grade school to graduate school, the need or expectation to hold a job that provides for growth and accomplishment increases systematically ($p < .01$). It would thus seem that the GNS is the result of a certain amount of social conditioning. The analysis of sex seems to affirm the normative nature of this variable; the ANOVA shows that male workers have a significantly higher growth need ($p < .01$) than do their female counterparts. However, males and females are equally satisfied with the opportunities for growth in the department. Male workers, however, expressed lower satisfaction with both job security and pay ($p < .01$) than did females. Our last analysis involved race. Black workers, regardless of sex, expressed lower growth-need strength or expectation ($p < .01$) than did the whites.

It seems clear from the data at hand that growth-need strength is a variable that varies to a significant degree as a function of the demographic characteristics of the workers. As we have seen, it is not systematically related to either the job characteristics or the outcome variables. To what extent growth need is, in fact, an expectation that is tempered and shaped by life experience remains yet to be determined. Given its significance as a moderator of satisfaction, more research similar to that initiated by Rosen (1959) and Turner and Lawrence (1965) seems in order.

A Final Look at Satisfaction

Exploration of the demographic correlates of growth-need strength suggested that it might be useful to look at the relationship between worker characteristics and the job outcomes. We therefore decided to compare worker-centered variables (demographic data) with job-centered variables (job dimensions) and see which set better predicted the job outcomes of the Hackman and Oldham model.

To do this, we separated the data pool into two major groups of predictors. The first group, the core job dimensions, represents the internal characteristics of a job as measured by the Job Diagnostic Survey. The second group consists of the personal history variables contained in the first section of the Job Analysis Survey. The outcome measures of internal work motivation, general satisfaction, and the five specific satisfactions were set up as criterion variables. For each of the seven criteria, we calculated two multiple-regression schemes— one for each class of predictor. The results of these calculations are presented in Table 5.7. Within each cell are the zero-order correlations,

TABLE 5.7
Comparison of Predictive Power of Job Characteristics and Worker Characteristics

	Work Outcomes	JDS Satisfaction Measures					
Predictors	General Satisfaction	Pay	Job Security	Social	Supervision	Opportunity for Growth	Internal Work Motivation
Core Job Dimensions, Internal Characteristics							
Variety	.24	-.02	.12	.11	.05	.35	.20
Identity	.19	.10	.05	.06	.08	.05	.07
Significance	.21	.05	.11	.16	.10	.24	.21
Autonomy	.30	.13	.23	.30	.13	.47	.19
Feedback: Job	.34	.06	.15	.16	.18	.33	.28
Feedback: Agents	.27	.03	.12	.20	.52	.22	.17
Dealing with Others	.06	.02	.08	.01	.02	.13	.07
R^a	.49	.17	.26	.34	.54	.58	.36
Worker Characteristics							
Age	.20	.22	.16	.22	.20	.27	.23
Sex	.04	.23	.12	.07	-.04	.03	.05
Educational Level	-.02	.01	.02	-.11	-.11	-.05	-.08
Experience (in Department)	.09	.19	.18	.03	.02	.20	.13
Time (on job)	.04	.14	.08	.05	.01	.15	.09
Race	.00	-.04	-.05	-.05	-.04	-.05	-.01
Growth-Need Strength	.03	-.07	-.12	.13	.07	.02	.02
R^a	.22	.34	.27	.28	.25	.28	.22

[a]These are "shrunken" multiple-correlation coefficients. All are significantly greater than zero ($p < .05$).

and in the two bottom rows are the multiple correlations (R) resulting from the regression equations.

The best way to interpret these data is to evaluate them against those in Table 5.5. That table presents the MPS correlations with these same work outcomes. In a sense, these correlations are analogous to multiple correlations, since the MPS formula combines the various job dimensions into a composite index. The total sample correlations in Table 5.5 can thus be compared to the multiple correlations for the core job dimensions in Table 5.7. Such an inspection show that the MPS index does a good job of capturing the predictive power of the job attributes. The multiple-regression equations generate a higher multiple correlation in most cases, but it should be remembered that such equations capitalize on situational variance in the sample. It is likely that cross validation with a new sample would result in even greater shrinkage than in the present situation. Table 5.7 also shows that the internal attributes of a job are generally better predictors of work outputs than are the personal characteristics of workers. As we have already said, some of the personal data, such as age and sex, show strong relationships with attitudes toward several specific sources of satisfaction. In general, however, the multiple correlations are lower ($p < .05$) than for the other set of variables.

SUMMARY

The analysis in this chapter concentrated on establishing the validity of the Job Diagnostic Survey and on testing the model formulated by Hackman and Oldham. In general, the data held up well on both counts.

First, we evaluated the concurrent validity of the core job dimensions measured by the JDS. We were interested in seeing whether differences in these dimensions were sensitive to differences in task content as established by the JAS job groups and families. This is indeed the case; the five job families formed in the subgrouping have distinctly different job dimensions. Furthermore, the pattern of differences is orderly in that it corresponds closely to the job progression set up under the departmental job classification scheme. This same order is reflected in the motivating potential score. This index, roughly corresponding to the capacity of the job to impart responsibility and be meaningful to the incumbent, increases systematically from family 1 through family 5. Thus, it seems that the core job dimensions are sensitive not only to categorical differences (nominal discrimination) but also to hierarchical differences (ordinal discrimination).

Because we had data from several independent sources, we were able to test several parts of the JDS. A number of subject matter experts rated the 77 tasks contained in the JAS. From these ratings, an importance index was generated for each job group and family. Given their definitions, the importance index and the motivating potential score should have been related, and they were. The observed Pearson coefficient of .83 between the two variables strongly enhances the validity of each. The subject matter experts also rated the tasks for Discretion. The JDS contains what ought to be a parallel measure of Autonomy. When these were correlated, the results (r = .80) again support the validity of each measure.

A considerable effort focused on the testing of the Hackman and Oldham central thesis, that workers who are placed in jobs suited to their need for growth and enrichment (high or low) will be more satisfied and motivated than workers who are mismatched in this regard. Generally speaking, the results bear this out. When the total sample is used, the proposition is supported by six of the seven work outcomes.

The nature of the growth-need strength variable, which is an important moderator variable in this reactive process, is not yet clear. It is obviously a personal attribute or mental set, since it is associated with differences in worker background and personal history.

All in all, the sense of order conveyed by the JAS data is not disturbed by the findings generated with the Job Diagnostic Survey. Our understanding of the dynamics of public sector employment has been increased. One gets the distinct impression, however, that both the JAS and the JDS only convey part of the picture of organizational life in a welfare department. All studies, however ambitious, have some limitations, and this project is no different. What is missing is an overview of the department as a bureaucracy and the relationship between that entity and the expectations of social workers as professionals. Furthermore, no data about numbers and types of clients served by these workers were included, and so we can only speculate about reactions to the human needs and problems with which workers must deal on a daily basis. These gaps in data and shortcomings in method do not prevent us from taking stock of where we are and where we need to go. In the final chapter, we will discuss the implications of our work and suggest some fruitful areas for further research.

NOTES

1. Values of this index can range from 1.00 to 343. See Chapter 4 for the details of its calculation.

2. See Chapter 3, Table 3.6, for a summary of the results of this process.

6
Implications

As of 1980, approximately 375,000 positions with social work designations could be found in 48,000 social agencies throughout the Unite States National Association of Social Workers (1980). Despite this tremendous investment in human capital, relatively little systematic research has focused on the exact nature of the work performed and the inherent characteristics of the social technology used within this massive industry. In preceding chapters, we have described data gathered as part of an ambitious study carried out in one public welfare setting. In this final chapter, we will discuss some of the implications of those data. As we shall see, some findings will be useful because they increase our understanding of social work practice within public welfare. Others will be useful because they are suggestive of new directions and further research.

SOCIAL WORK PRACTICE IN A BUREAUCRACY

Scope and Diversity

At the time of this study, the Alabama Department of Pensions and Security (DPS) was administering a full range of federal and state programs involving public assistance, social services, and an array of medical, employment-related, and nutritional programs. To manage this fragmented configuration, the department had become a bureaucracy in the classical sense of the term; it possessed a complex division of labor, an explicit hierarchy of authority, specialization, proliferation of written rules, and a career ladder for its workers. Many of the salient characteristics of the job activities in the department seem to flow from that fact. Let us illustrate the point.

One of the clear impressions conveyed by the data is the diverse activity encompassed by the jobs contained in the social work series. Although they are packaged in an orderly classification scheme, these jobs seem to reflect the fact that social work in the public sector may have survived the 1960s as much by accumulation as by evolution. What has emerged into the 1980s, at least in this organization, looks very much like the "hybrid organization" of Wilensky (1964) and the "semi-profession" of Toren (1969). Whatever we choose to call it, the job activities require a wide range of therapeutic, interpersonal, adaptive, legal, and organizational skills. As will soon be seen, this breadth and diffuseness will have important implications for the preparation of workers in both university-based and in-service training programs, as well as for the proprietary hold that social work has traditionally exercised over these many positions.

Indirect Practice Orientation

Another striking characteristic of the job activity in the DPS is its orientation toward indirect practice. A sizeable proportion of the workers are engaged in some form of organizational maintenance or support activity. The largest single job family in the sample, the Eligibility Workers, make up one-third of the sample. They are responsible for screening clients at intake and determining eligibility for services, in-kind programs, and financial assistance. Although some assessment of service needs is carried out, the raison d'être of this group is clearly client surveillance. This function, mandated by a host of program requirements, occupies a considerable portion of the labor force in the department. Two other groups, almost 26 percent of the sample, have little or no direct contact with clients on a regular basis. Of these, 13 percent are supervisors and another 13 percent are administrators of various programs and departments.

The remaining two job families, the Human Services Workers and the Social Service Workers, constitute the direct service cadre of the department. Of these, however, the Social Service Workers make up only 26 percent of the sample. This may contribute to the cognitive dissonance between public welfare and the social work profession. Only this small cadre, far less than a majority, conforms to the practitioner image that social work has of itself. Even this function is blurred by the sine qua non of the bureaucratic presence—paperwork.

The profile of the social service worker (see Figure 3.4) reflects one of the highest loadings in Paper Flow of all the job families.

Other Practice Characteristics

Before leaving this characterization of practice, several other summary points are in order. The first concerns specialization. Of the five job families defined in the study, three (the Human Service Workers, Eligibility Workers, and Supervisors) are highly specialized. They represent a functional specialization, that is, specialization by activity. The Social Service Workers, while seeming to have a broader array of functions, are actually specialized by program area or client type. The service generalist, as characterized by the SREB material of Teare and McPheeters (1970) is conspicuous by its absence.

The predominant mode of intervention is individualized casework. Work with groups (other than families) and community organization are rarely engaged in. The data also show that a relatively low priority is placed on advocacy or on any agressive attempt to bring about changes in the service or structural patterns of the department. Reaching out to people who are at risk is also not an autonomous part of institutionalized practice. These last practice attributes seem to be the residue of a lingering belief in the case poverty concept referred to in Chapter 1—the historic perception that poverty is related solely to the individual and his or her preparation and functioning. With this as an implicit philosophy, little emphasis is likely to be placed on system change. Furthermore, it is a rare bureaucracy that will encourage its employees to bite the hand that feeds them. This agency is no different in that regard.

THE DILEMMA OF INSTITUTIONALIZED SERVICE

As we discussed in Chapters 3 through 5, there is an orderliness inherent in the activities carried out within the DPS.[1] There is also a systematic pattern reflected by the workers' self-reported characterizations of their jobs. The core dimensions that contribute to meaningfulness, responsibility, and motivating potential increase as one moves up the job ladder in the social worker series.

This neat progression is not repeated by the data on job satisfaction. First, we hasten to point out that few people in the department reported real dissatisfaction; few of the means for any of the workers fell below the neutral category.[2] Nevertheless, workers in two job families, the Eligibility Workers and the Social Service Workers, consistently reported lower values on almost all satisfaction measures. The analysis of growth-need strength as a moderator of satisfaction clearly indicated that this variable cannot be offered as an explanation for the relatively low level of satisfaction of these two families (see Table 5.6). At this point, a tentative explanation can be offered only by speculating about factors not measured by the two instruments used in the study.

Evidence is beginning to accumulate indicating that the amount and kind of client contact is an important determinant of worker response. Three of the five JAS families have job activities that require continuous direct contact with clients—the Human Services Workers, the Eligibility Workers, and the Social Service Workers. Unlike the other two, however, job satisfaction among the Human Services Workers is high. We believe this group is unique for a number of reasons. First, this is a functionally specialized group. These paraprofessionals spend most of their time providing personal care to clients in their own homes. In addition, they perform chores and instruct the clients in daily living skills. In short, they provide tangible, discrete, direct services to their clients. Furthermore, at the time of the data collection, the Homemaker Services Program was just getting under way. Most of the contacts with these workers gave us the distinct impression of the sort of cohesiveness and high morale one would expect from a new endeavor. Because the program was new, workers were encouraged to suggest changes and to work closely with supervision. By the same token, the program's newness may have contributed to a sense of uncertainty about its future. The pattern of satisfaction means for this job family tends to support these impressions.

The Eligibility Workers and Social Service Workers are different. They are working in older programs, with complicated, well-entrenched policies. Many Eligibility Workers are assigned to income maintenance programs and to screening clients for benefits. The social Service Workers do not have a discrete, circumscribed array of duties. Both groups continually strive to meet a wider array of physical and emotional needs than their resources will permit. Both manage large case loads (Case Management, Specific) and have a heavy involvement in paperwork (Paper Flow).

Our speculation is that the low satisfaction of these two job families may be caused by the dilemma of trying to maintain accountability while fostering a climate of service. Recent work in the area of "burnout" and occupational tedium have shown that variables such as case-load characteristics and paperwork significantly influence social workers' attitudes toward their jobs (Pines and Kafrey 1978). Other researchers (Forbes 1973; Kroeger 1971) have shown that workers, especially caseworkers, develop systematic orientations over time to help them reconcile the inconsistencies associated with serving the public in a welfare context. To paraphrase Street, Martin, and Gordon (1979), it may well be that the tension induced by the expectation of giving (service norm), coupled with the expectation of taking away (surveillance norm), is particularly acute for these two groups of workers. Unfortunately, our data do not permit much more than speculation about these phenomena at the present time.[3]

SOME PROBLEMS RESULTING FROM THE DIVISION OF LABOR

Mobility within the Organization

As we have seen, most jobs in the department are of a specialized nature. The form may vary from level to level, but specialization is the rule rather than the exception. This division of labor results in practice areas that are disjointed conceptually but represent the paths along which people move as they progress through the job hierarchy of the department. The transition from services through supervision to administration involves a considerable shift in subject matter and skill.

This basic discontinuity can cause real problems for agency administrators. As a rule, organizational advancement requires that people move from clinical to indirect service positions. This is certainly true of the jobs in the social worker series in this agency. A person capable of carrying out the diverse functions required by this progression is rare. This makes it difficult for an agency administrator who wants to reward good workers with promotions but still retain a competent work force of clinicians and supervisors.

Establishing the Relevance of Credentials

The prevalence of specialization within the department suggest that there may be problems with regard to the job relatedness of many social work curricula. Here we will draw from survey data recently compiled by Dinerman (forthcoming).[4] Her data suggest that most undergraduate programs are organized around some sort of generic principle. Whatever the organizing principle, the attempt seems to be to train for breadth rather than for depth. Given the diverse range of duties workers are called upon to perform, this may not be a bad strategy, but it does raise the risk of graduates who are unable to master any of them. Most programs have practice components that are heavily weighted toward beginning casework. As mentioned earlier, only 27 percent of the workers in our sample were engaged in this type of activity.

A similar problem may exist with graduate education. In the study sample, 66 percent of the supervisors and administrators have the MSW degree and 96 percent have at least some graduate education in social work. Graduate training is a requirement for most of these positions. We have every reason to believe that the DPS is typical in this respect. Despite this, there seems to be relatively little emphasis placed on preparation for this type of work at the graduate level. Richan and Mendelsohn (1973) present data showing that, in 1970, only 2 percent of the students enrolled in graduate social work programs had selected administration as an area of concentration. Dinerman's data, collected almost a decade later, suggest that things may not be much different. The graduate programs she surveyed varied greatly in organizing themes and in the practice options offered as majors and minors. There is also a clear indication that direct practice and casework still predominated as areas of concentration.

Given the nature of work as revealed by this study, these characteristics of social work education should cause concern if the social work profession wishes to maintain its position as the driving force in the welfare industry. (In this sample, only 42 percent of the workers have specialized social work education, but, as we have seen, agency management consists almost exclusively of social workers.) Under the Uniform Guidelines on Employee Selection Procedures (Equal Employment Opportunity Commission 1978), if a minimum requirement for employment has an adverse impact on minorities or other protected groups (and most credentials do), an employer must demonstrate the job relatedness of such a requirement, which means establishing its validity. At present, criterion-referenced validation strategies are plagued with technical problems, and content validation strategies, particularly for credentials, need to be developed (Feild and Teare 1980; Teare and Feild 1980). In the not too distant future, however, it is likely that social work eduation will be called upon to validate its claim to this occupational "turf." Given the apparent diversity in program content and the lack of unifying principles, this may prove to be difficult.

CONCLUDING COMMENTS

In the latter chapters of this book, a clear picture of the DPS as an organized bureaucracy begins to take shape. We choose not to label that picture as either positive or negative but rather as an accurate reflection of the way things are. The problems and dilemmas raised by the findings strongly reinforce the call made by Thomas (1978) for a developmental research thrust within social work. A wide range of fundamental issues needs to be addressed. For example, if specialization is to be the hallmark of professionals within organizations, we need to know more about the appropriate dimensions on which to base specilization (for example, by function, by problem type, by client type). Clearly, no consistency is to be found in either the educational or occupational domain; formulation of curricular specilities is usually made without regard to the way the labor is divided in a particular job market.

If we are going to promote people from clinical to administrative positions, we need to identify linkage skills between the two domains so that we can do a better job of selecting managers. By the same token, if highly skilled and motivated clinicians are going to choose to remain in place rather than move up the ladder, we need better rationales for work assignments that take full advantage of their expertise. At present, no clear guidelines exist on how to identify difficult or complex cases or even on what an appropriate case load should be.

We need to know more about occupational tedium and "burnout" —especially how it can be prevented. If it can be dealt with through structural changes or by redesigning jobs, we should investigate these options. Periodic treatment through talk sessions or quasi-therapeutic counseling programs are palliative at best.

Finally, there is a need for social work and public welfare to examine their relationship. Neither can afford to view the other with disdain. Only the helping professions, especially social work, can assist this massive national industry in avoiding the mistakes of the production industries. Davis and Taylor (1972) warned about the mindless application of efficiency and methods engineering to service organizations. When we are harried by cries either for efficiency or for reform, we would do well to heed their words:

Disturbingly, while the trend toward post-industrial organization is growing, the task and job rationalization mode is being imported with untutored disregard into the social service sector—to that sector's considerable peril (p. 18).

NOTES

1. The department has since redefined its classification scheme to incorporate some of the findings of this study. The Reviewer classification was eliminated, and those incumbents were reclassified by function. Two additional social worker classes were added to permit clinical specialization. Classifications with few incumbents were eliminated and combined with existing ones.

2. At present, most standardized scales lack normative data on the job attitudes of professional workers. This is especially true of the Job Diagnostic Survey. Consequently, we really do not know the extent to which this type of worker will express dissatisfaction. The limited data available suggest that mean satisfaction values for service workers may be consistently higher than those for production workers.

3. We intend to explore these relationships further. As of this writing, we are compiling data from a public welfare setting in another region. These data include measures of job content and characteristics, supervisory style, case-load size and characteristics, worker demography, and satisfaction.

4. Some care should be taken in making broad generalizations from Dinerman's data. Her sample covers 20 percent of the independent undergraduate programs, 20 percent of the jointly administered graduate-undergraduate programs, and 20 percent of the independent MSW programs.

Appendix A:
Summary Descriptions
of Major Job Classifications
in the Social Worker Series

Human Services Aide I: This is entry-level work in performing a variety of supportive services to the disadvantaged. Employees are selected for their interest and aptitude for work of this nature and are placed in a formal training program conducted and approved by the state agency concerned. Emphasis in the training is on the development of basic knowledge, skills, abilities, and attitudes necessary to provide supportive services to clients. Training and work assignments are performed under close supervision.

Human Services Aide II: This is nonprofessional work in performing a variety of supportive services to the disadvantaged. Employees in this class provide a variety of routine outreach or support services to clients. Work involves providing general information and assistance to those in need by acting as a communications link with the grant-in-aid agency to which assigned. Some supervision and guidance may be given to employees in a lower class for training and initial work assignments. Employees work under the close supervision of an employee of higher rank, who provides detailed instructions for work assignments.

Human Services Aid III: This is nonprofessional work of an advanced and supervisory nature in performing a variety of supportive services to the disadvantaged. Employees in this class follow standard but moderately complex routines in providing a variety of outreach or supportive services to clients. Work usually involves the supervision of a few aides of lower classes. Employees use their own initiative in the solution of most day-to-day problems; however, assistance from professional superiors is available. Work is performed with considerable independence but is reviewed on a regular basis.

Public Assistance Eligibility Technician: This is technical work in the administration and management of financial assistance to individual applicants. Employees in this class are responsible for making determinations of eligibility of applicants and redetermination of eligibility of recipients for financial assistance, Medicaid, and food stamp programs. Work involves analyzing data gathered by interviewing applicants and their relatives, investigating financial sources by checking public records and contacting various individuals and organizations, and examining case material. Employees complete necessary forms and assistance data in terms of the agency standards for the particular category. Employees prepare budgets and make eligibility determinations for financial assistance, Medicaid, and food stamp programs. Employees advise applicants and recipients of available services and make referrals to the agency's social service unit. Employees are guided by manuals of procedure, by bulletins and letters of instruction, and by supervisory conferences and review of employees' records. Employees are subject to internal checks for compliance with governing laws and agency standards.

Casework Reviewer: This is professional social work in the field of public welfare. Employees in this class are responsible for reviewing the processes and validity of case actions by local agencies in connection with the determination of eligibility for money payment and other services in the federally matched categories; supervising the total operation of a local food stamp program; evaluating case material to determine the quality and accuracy of local agency decisions on approval or denial of applications, redeterminations of eligibility, and discontinuance of assistance; assisting in the analysis of findings to identify sources of problems; recommending need for services in accordance with state plan requirements; and recommending appropriate corrective measures. The information secured is used by administrative staff in developing more effective operations. Employees make home visits to clients and necessary collateral contacts. Employees may supervise a small professional and clerical staff. Employees are expected to work with considerable initiative and independence in planning and conducting studies and making reports and recommendations. Their work is usually reviewed by a supervisor to assure conformity with agency policy and requirements.

Social Worker I: This is entry-level professional social work involving children, youths, and adults. Employees in this class are responsible for determining applicant's eligibility and need for social services, for developing a social service plan for each case, and for providing direct delivery or referral services that assure attainment of mutually established client goals. Work includes assessment of the need and delivery of services such as day care, employment and job training referral, family counseling, certain protective services, foster care, certain adoption services, recruitment and supervision of foster and day care homes, follow-up services for crippled children, arranging for guardianship or other protective placement, arranging for clinical services, planning for nursing home care, and enabling persons to remain or return to their own homes. Work is guided by a manual of procedure, by bulletins and letters of instruction, and by regular conferences with supervisors. General quality of work is determined through periodic review of case records and reports by professional supervisors.

Social Worker II: This is responsible, advanced professional social work involving children, youths, and adults. Employees in this class are responsible for the performance of those duties assigned to Social Workers I; however, they are expected to exhibit a higher degree of skill and discretion in determining services needed and method of delivery. The differentiating factor involves the higher degree of social and psychological dysfunctioning and complexity of behavioral problems of the client with whom the social worker will be expected to deal. Work is guided by manuals of procedures, by bulletins and letters of instructions, and by conferences with supervisors. General quality of work is determined primarily through periodic review of case records and intermittent review of case-load reports by professional supervisors.

Casework Supervisor: This is professional and supervisory social work in directing a group of caseworkers in a large rural county or a metropolitan area. Employees in this class supervise, review, and coordinate the work of a group of workers engaged in providing casework services to public welfare clients. Work includes responsibility for training inexperienced caseworkers and child welfare workers in the principles and techniques of professional social work. In some instances employees may carry small case loads, usually consisting of complicated service or child welfare cases. Work may involve assisting a county director on program administrative problems and providing public interpretation of welfare services.

County Welfare Director I: This is social service work of an administrative nature in directing the welfare department activities in a county where the case load requires only a small professional and clerical staff. Employees in this class are responsible for supervising a program providing casework services to public welfare clients. Because of the limited professional staff, these employees often personally carry case loads, usually consisting of child welfare or more difficult service cases. Work involves responsibility for program coordination with other social agencies in the county, contacts with local professional and civic groups, and development of improved service by the agency. Although the county director is appointed by the county welfare board, administrative responsibility is to the state department. Technical direction, advice, and consultation on program policy, procedure, and casework or administrative problems are given by representatives of the state department.

County Welfare Director II: This is social service of an administrative nature in directing or assisting in directing the welfare department activities in a county where the case load necessitates a moderate to large professional, clerical, and supporting staff. Employees in this class are responsible for administering or assisting in administering a program providing casework services to public welfare clients. The emphasis of this work is on administrative matters, although the employee may frequently be called on to review difficult cases and to give direction as to the most effective procedures to be used. Work may involve serving as assistant to a county director of a large urban county. In a county where there is no Casework Supervisor, the employee may share responsibility for giving detailed technical supervision to caseworkers and child welfare workers. Work involves responsibility for program coordination with other social agencies in the county, development of improved service by the agency, and stimulation of interest and understanding of the program among county professional and civic groups. Although the county director is appointed by the county welfare board, administrative responsibility is to the state department. Technical direction, advice, and consultation on program policy, procedure, and administrative problems are given by representatives of the state department.

County Welfare Director III: This is social service work of an administrative nature in directing or assisting in the administration of the welfare department activities in a county where the case load necessitates a large professional, clerical, and supporting staff. Employees in this class are responsible for the administering or assisting in the administration of a program providing casework services to public welfare clients. Although employees may review and make recommendations on more complex and difficult cases referred to them by the Casework Supervisor, the main emphasis of the work is on administrative matters. Work involves responsibility for development of improved service by the agency, coordination of the program with other welfare services in the county, and stimulation of interest and understanding of the program among county professional and civic groups. Work may also involve serving as assistant to a county director of a large metropolitan county. Although the county director is appointed by the county welfare board, administrative responsibility is to the state department. Technical direction, advice, and consultation on program policy, procedure, and administrative problems are given by representatives of the state department.

County Welfare Director IV: This is social service work of an administrative nature in directing the welfare department activities in a large metropolitan county. Employees in this class are responsible for administration of a program providing casework services to public welfare clients in a county where the case load necessitates a large clerical, professional, and supervisory staff. Employees are mainly responsible for the application of program knowledge and administrative techniques to varied and complex problems of public relations, correlation of agency services with other agencies' work, and proper attainment of technical objectives of the various programs. Detailed supervisory duties are delegated to professional and clerical supervisors, but the employee gives general direction to the various clerical and social work functions performed. Although the county director is appointed by the county welfare board, administrative responsibility is to the state department. Technical direction, advice, and consultation on program policy, procedure, and administrative problems are given by representatives of the state department.

County Welfare Director V: This is social service work of an administrative nature in directing the welfare department activities in the largest metropolitan county. Employees in this class are responsible for administration of a program providing casework services to public welfare clients in a county where the case load necessitates a large clerical, professional, and supervisory staff. The employee is mainly responsible for the application of program knowledge and administrative techniques to varied and complex problems of public relations, correlation of agency services with other agencies' work, and proper attainment of technical objectives of the various programs. Detailed supervisory duties are delegated to professional and clerical supervisors, but the employee gives general direction to the various clerical and social work functions performed. Although the county director is appointed by the county welfare board, administrative responsibility is to the state department. Technical direction, advice, and consultation on program policy, procedure, and administrative problems is given by representatives of the state department.

Welfare Administrator I: This is professional and administrative social work involving the direction of service activities or the supervision of personnel training programs. Work is usually performed as assistant to an administrative superior. Employees assist in the formulation of standards of casework services and give working supervision to other staff members who are rendering consultative services. Although work is under the general supervision of a public welfare executive, who makes final determinations on major policy matters, employees have considerable responsibility for the planning, development, and efficient functioning of a social service program at the division level. Employees may be assigned supervisory responsibility for one or more areas of the social service program.

Welfare Administrator II: This is professional social service work of an administrative nature in directing a major bureau of the state welfare program. Employees in this class are responsible for planning, organizing, and coordinating activities and for maintaining acceptable standards of social service in such bureaus as public assistance and adult services, research and statistics, family and children services, or field service. Work involves appraising the effectiveness of the programs and recommending new methods to bring about improvement in services. Although assignments are made in broad outline and work must be conducted in accordance with departmental policies and standards, employees exercise some degree of administrative independence.

Welfare Supervisor I: This is professional social work of a consultive, technical, or administrative nature. Employees in this class have responsibility for developing uniform interpretations and explanations of policies and procedures for the county departments and for providing consultative services to them. Employees may work in adoption services, emergency welfare services, licensing of child-care institutions, special programs and projects service, or performance of specialized services, such as aid in administering the service programs or income maintenance programs.

Welfare Supervisor II: This is advanced professional social work in the administration and supervision of a public welfare program. Employees in this class may be responsible for planning, supervising, and coordinating a public welfare program in an assigned area, for conducting a staff-development program in a large urban area, or for developing and interpreting policies for the administration of the income maintenance program. Work involves acting as liaison between the state and county departments, with responsibility for seeing that policies, procedures, and standards of assistance and service are applied uniformly. Duties are performed in accordance with accepted regulations and well-defined procedures, but employees exercise independent judgment in applying standard policies to specific situations.

Welfare Supervisor III: This is responsible, professional social work in the administration of a specific phase of a public assistance or child welfare program in an assigned area of the state. Employees assist administrators in formulating workable procedures for implementing policies and have responsibility for interpreting policies and procedures. Employees in this class may have responsibility for one of the major programs of child welfare services throughout the state, such as adoption and foster home services, licensing of child-care agencies, and consultant services to local child welfare workers. Work is conducted in accordance with accepted regulations and well-defined procedures, but employees exercise considerable independent judgment in applying standard policies to specific situations.

Emergency Welfare Services Supervisor: This is professional social work involved with the development and administration of plans to assure continuity of public assistance programs under disaster conditions. Employees in this class coordinate civil defense welfare services with other public and private welfare agencies at all levels and with other civil defense services. They assist in formulating workable procedures for implementing policies and procedures in the area of civil defense. Employees work under the general direction of the director of the Bureau of Informational Service. Work is conducted in accordance with accepted regulations and procedures, but employees exercise independent judgment in applying standard policies to specific situations.

Appendix B:
Initial Version of
the Job Analysis Survey
(Used January to March 1975)

<u>Description of Questionnaire</u>

This Questionnaire is designed to provide an overview description of your job activities. Properly answered, it should reflect what you are actually doing in the position you fill. PLEASE, indicate what you are actually doing. Do not be concerned that this may not be what your job specification says you should be doing.

The Questionnaire consists of three parts. Part I requests that you describe how your time is divided among a group of six job-task clusters. Each of these clusters are defined for you. Part II requests that you describe how your time is divided among thirty-two tasks. Part III requests some information about your overall or general job characteristics.

Job Title _____   County _____

JAS-75

113

Personal Information

The personal information requested here will be treated in the strictest confidence, and will be used only in achieving the goals and purposes of this survey. The number for the position you fill was randomly selected from a restricted sample. Your name and its use is limited to the data gathering portion of this survey effort and will be removed from the instrument upon receipt of the entire sample.

Name _____ Date _____

Location (County, Bureau, or Division) _____

Job Classification, i.e., SW I, CWR, etc. _____ Program Effort ____

Position, e.g., Intake, Supervisor County Food Stamp Office, etc. _____
_____

Age _____ Race _____ Sex _____

Education Level, for example, BA, BSW, or BA + 1 year graduate shcool, etc.
_____

Degree, year, and school _____

Undergraduate major/minor, and graduate major if appropriate _____
_____

Time (years/month) in present position. _____

Date of original appointment to the Department _____

2

Instructions for Completing Survey

IT IS ABSOLUTELY NECESSARY THAT YOU READ THROUGH THE ENTIRE
SURVEY BEFORE ATTEMPTING TO COMPLETE ANY SINGLE PART THEREOF. Feel
free to question the survey monitor concerning any definition or
question. Now begin to answer the survey questions in accordance with the
following instructions.

Part I – A Percentage of Time

1. Turn to the task cluster chart on page 4, Column I-A

2. Read the definitions for the six task clusters presented in
   the task cluster chart. For a complete understanding of the
   tasks within a cluster read through the task definitions found
   on pages 5 thru 10.

3. Now, think of your job.

4. Relate your work activities, in a typical month, to the defined
   task clusters. Now divided your job into the six clusters
   presented in the chart. Using 100% of your time as the total
   limit, assign a percentage of your work time to each cluster.
   If none of your time is spent in a particular task cluster, put
   a zero in column I-A beside that cluster's definition. Go back
   and forth and revise your percentageestimates as you find it
   necessary to do so.

5. Be sure the numbers (percentages) in column I-A add up to 100.
   Be sure there is a number in column I-A for each cluster.

Part I – B Amount of Freedom or Discretion – Indicates the degree to which
            you determine the if, when, or how of carrying out these tasks.

1. Turn to cluster chart on page 4, Column I-B.

2. Review the definitions of task clusters that you indicated in
   Part I-A were applicable to your job.

3. Levels of freedom and discretion to be used in this question are
   described as follows:

   A. Very little – almost never exercise any freedom or
      discretion in determining the if, when, or how to
      carry out these tasks.

   B. Little – seldom have any freedom or discretion in
      determining the if, when, or how to carry out these
      tasks.

   C. Some – about as often as not have freedom or dis-
      cretion in determining the if, when, or how to carry
      out these tasks.

   D. Much – most of the time have freedom or discretion
      in determining the if, when, or how to carry out
      these tasks.

E. Very much — almost always have freedom or
discretion in determining the if, when, or
how to carry out these tasks.

4. From the preceding descriptions of levels of discretion, select
the letter that relates to the level of discretion you exercise
in each cluster. Place that letter in the appropriate space of
column I-B of the chart.

Task Clusters (definitions)	I-A Percentage of time spent	I-B Amount of freedom or discretion
1. Direct Clinical — Activities re- lated directly to the providing of direct assistance or services to clients.		
2. Indirect Clinical — Activities related to developing resources or providing indirect services and assistance.		
3. Supervision — Activities related to the direction of work and/or workers (self as well as others.)		
4. Training — Activities realted to the teaching, instruction, and orientation of workers.		
5. Clerical — Activities related to the processing of written infor- mation and data.		
6. Administration — Activities re- lated to the management and di- rection of programs and/or other work units.		

Part II   Job Tasks

In Part I of this survey you assigned a percentage of your total work time to various job clusters. Now we want to find out in more detail how you spend your time within these job clusters. The following instructions will assist you in completing Part II of this survey. The first job cluster to be reviewed more thoroughly is the Direct Clinical.

1. Think of the Direct Clinical aspect of your job.

2. Review the definitions of all 13 sub-tasks of this cluster. These cover the range of Direct Clinical activities.

3. Using 100% as the limit, distribute the time spent in Direct Clinical tasks among these 13 sub-tasks. Keep in mind the 100% represents total time spent in the Direct Clinical cluster of tasks and not in the total job.

4. Assign a percentage of your Direct Clinical time, in A TYPICAL MONTH, to each of the 13 tasks. Before assigning any percentage figures, read all 13 tasks and eliminate those tasks you do not perform. On the Job Task Chart place a zero in % of TIME SPENT column beside those tasks you do not perform.

5. Use the coded descriptions of levels of discretion from Part I-B, pages 3 and 4, to indicate on the Job Task Chart the amount of freedom or discretion you exercise in determining the if, when, or how to carry out these sub-tasks.

6. Do not leave any blank spaces in the % of TIME SPENT column of the Job Task Chart.

A. Direct Clinical — Activities related directly to the providing of direct assistance or services to clients.

JOB TASK CHART

	% of time spent	Amount of freedom or discretion
1. Going out of the agency and into the community to try to find people who need services.		
2. Telling clients about the programs, services, and kinds of help your agency can give them.		
3. Giving clients advice about their problems and helping them plan and make decisions. (For example, about their family, jobs, or money.)		

		% of time spent	Amount of freedom or discretion
4.	Getting information from clients through interviews to find out the kinds of needs and problems they have.		
5.	Referring clients who need help to your agency or other agencies and following them up to make sure they get the help they need.		
6.	Doing homemaking and house-keeping tasks for clients. (For example, cleaning house, cooking, buying gro-ceries.)		
7.	Giving nursing and medical care. (For example, giving first aid, giving medicines, giving routine physical exam-inations.)		
8.	Giving personal care. (For example, helping people with grooming, bathing.)		
9.	Going with clients or taking clients to places where they can get help. (For example, taking clients or driving clients to places they need to go.)		
10.	Teaching clients how to do things for themselves. (For example, how to cook, sew, fix things around the house, take care of other members of the family.)		
11.	Administering tests and ex-aminations to clients. (For example, personality tests, or job preference tests.)		
12.	Interpreting test and exami-nation findings of clients. (For example, from personality tests, or job preference tests.)		
13.	Determining if clients are eligible to receive assistance and/or services from your agency.		

The directions on page 5 will also apply here
except that it is now the Indirect Clinical
aspect of your job that you are dividing.
Remember, review all the task definitions in
the cluster before deciding on a division of
your time among the tasks.

B. Indirect Clinical - Activities related to developing resources or
providing indirect services and assistance.

	% of time spent	Amount of freedom or discretion
1. Finding resources and sources of help for clients. (For example, finding people who will give furniture, clothing, food, medicine or money to clients, finding foster homes, finding day care facilities, finding jobs for clients.)		
2. Consulting with, advising, or giving assistance to people (or groups) within or outside of the agency.		
3. Mobilizing people (or groups) to do something about problems in the community. (For example, organizing a group of clients, getting PTA or church groups to contribute money, time, or space, getting business people involved in social services.)		
4. Trying to get rules, laws, policies, or practices changed when they keep clients from getting services or prevent workers from carrying out jobs.		
5. Making speeches or giving talks to different groups of people in the community about problems in the community. (For example, talking to PTA, Jaycees, church clubs, high school classes.)		

7

The directions on page 5 will also apply here
except that it is now the Supervisory aspect
of your job that you are dividing.

C. Supervision — Activities related to the direction of work and/or workers
    (self as well as others).

	% of time spent	Amount of freedom or discretion
1. Caseload Management. (Activities associated with scheduling, co-ordinating, and planning for the management of a caseload.)		
2. Case Study. (Study and analysis of case materials for familiarization purposes in new assignments or prior to client contact (for case management).		
3. Case Review. Monitoring records preparation, checking for adequacy of records, and for proper services and assistance.		
4. Evaluating Workers. (For example, observing worker performance, filling out performance appraisals, giving feedback and guidance.)		
5. Interpreting and Explaining Policy Materials. (For example, explaining or clarifying program regulations. DPS policy guides, HEW or USDA directives to any or all levels of agency personnel or clients.)		
6. Assigning Work Tasks or Cases. (For example, assigning new cases to workers, making out work schedules for staff.)		

8

The directions on page 5 will also apply here
except that it is now the Training aspect of
your job that you are dividing.

D. Training – Activities related to the teaching, instruction, and
orientation of workers.

	% of time spent	Amount of freedom or discretion
1. Teaching workers job skills. (For example, telling or showing workers how to carry out an interview, prepare a budget, assess service needs, or other job-related skills.)		

The directions on page 5 will also apply here
except that it is now the Clerical aspect of
your job that you are dividing.

E. Clerical – Activities related to the processing of written
information and data.

	% of time spent	Amount of freedom or discretion
1. Carrying out clerical tasks. (For example, filling out forms, requisitions, filing materials, writing letters.)		
2. Case recording. (Preparing, updating, proofreading the narrative portion of the case record.)		

9

The directions on page 5 will also apply here
except that it is now the Administrative aspect
of your job that you are dividing.

F. Administration – Activities related to the management and direction
                    of programs and/or other work units.

	% of time spent	Amount of freedom or discretion
1. Reading & reviewing policy materials. (For example, keeping abreast of program instructions or regulations, administrative letters, SRS and HEW guidelines, USDA directives, manual revisions.)		
2. Planning agency programs or projects that have to do either with the community, clients, or workers. (For example, planning a "hot meal" program for children, planning a training program for new workers.)		
3. Helping your agency decide if a program or project dealing with the community, clients, or workers is successful or not.		
4. Monitoring the environment. (For example, keeping track of inventory, supplies, resources or insuring that buildings or working areas are safe, secure and clean.)		

10

Part III The following are questions about your job and your work <u>in</u>
          <u>general</u>. Please circle the number which best fits your answer.

1. In general, how much <u>freedom</u> do you have in doing your job?
   1. Very little   4. Much
   2. Little   5. Very much
   3. Some

2. Looking at your job as a whole, how <u>helpful</u> is it to your clients?
   1. Never helpful   4. Often helpful
   2. Rarely helpful   5. Very much
   3. Sometimes helpful

3. Considering everything about your job, how <u>important</u> is it to
   your agency?
   1. Not at all important   4. Important
   2. Of very little importance   5. Very important
   3. Somewhat important

4. Within a 40-hour week how many hours are devoted to activities
   <u>that</u> <u>you</u> <u>decide</u> require your involvement? For instance, how
   many hours a week are you free to devote to activities <u>of your</u>
   <u>choice</u>. (Your involvement in these activities is not a result
   of supervisory direction or suggestion, nor of felt obligation
   to other workers. The activities <u>can</u> include tasks found in
   this survey.
   1. None
   2. Less than one-hour-a-day   4. Two-hours-a-day
   3. One-hour-a-day   5. Three-hours-a-day
                                     6. Four-hours-a-day

5. If in question four you indicated that you do have some free
   time to devote to activities of your choice, please indicate
   here some examples of these activities:

11

6. As part of your job, how <u>often</u> do you come in contact with the following type of people? Please <u>circle</u> the number that <u>best</u> fits your answer.

TYPES OF PEOPLE	NEVER	SELDOM	SOMETIMES	OFTEN	VERY OFTEN
Your supervisor	1	2	3	4	5
Doctors, nurses	1	2	3	4	5
Police	1	2	3	4	5
Ministers, priests	1	2	3	4	5
Lawyers or judges	1	2	3	4	5
Parole Officers	1	2	3	4	5
Personnel from other agencies (counselors, food stamp)	1	2	3	4	5
Director of your department	1	2	3	4	5
Clients	1	2	3	4	5
Members of clients' family	1	2	3	4	5
Community officials (eg., mayors, city councilmen)	1	2	3	4	5
Volunteer Groups (eg., PTA, Church, Lions)	1	2	3	4	5
Business leaders	1	2	3	4	5

7. In the space provided, please add any other comments you feel are pertinent to the purpose and objectives of this survey.

Other comments:

Appendix C:
Final Version of
the Job Analysis Survey
(Used February to April 1976)

This Questionnaire is the second in a series designed to provide up-to-date information about your job activities. Properly answered, it should reflect what you are actually doing in your present job and will help the Department to develop an accurate classification of jobs and job duties.

The Questionnaire has three parts. Part I requests that you describe how frequently you carry out specific tasks. Part II involves indicating how much of your time is divided among a group of 8 job-task clusters. Each cluster is defined for you. Part III asks for information about general characteristics of your job.

Read over each part entirely before answering any of the questions in them. Feel free to question the survey monitor about definitions or any items that are not clear. Be sure to also read the instructions in the JOB ANALYSIS SURVEY Booklet which accompanies this questionnaire. It will help you to record your answers more quickly and accurately.

Job Title _____   County _____

-1-

PERSONAL INFORMATION

The information about yourself that is requested below will be treated in the strictest confidence. No data will be reported to the Department of Pensions and Security in ways that will involve the use of your name or other identifying data. This information is being obtained to avoid duplication during data collection and analysis. In filling out this page, please follow the instructions contained in the JOB ANALYSIS SURVEY Booklet on pages 1 through 4.

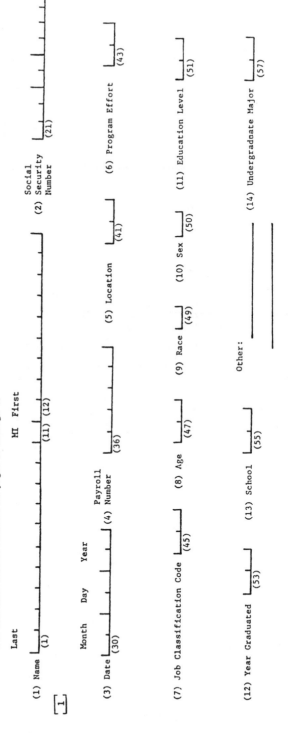

(1) Name _____
     Last   MI   First

(2) Social Security Number

[1]

(3) Date _____
     Month Day Year

(4) Payroll Number

(5) Location

(6) Program Effort

(7) Job Classification Code

(8) Age

(9) Race

(10) Sex

(11) Education Level

(12) Year Graduated

(13) School

(14) Undergraduate Major

Other: _____

(15) Time (years) in present position

(16) Date of Original Appointment to Department

     Month Year

-2-

PART I - FREQUENCY OF ACTIVITY

In this part of the SURVEY, we are interested in getting more detailed information about your job. Instructions for entering answers for this section can be found starting on page 4 of the SURVEY Booklet. Please turn to that section and read over the scales contained in it.

As you go through Part I, read each of the tasks in the Task Clusters. Decide if you do it or not. Using the scale in the Booklet, mark how often you do it in the course of a typical month in Column A. If you never do it, leave the box in Column B blank. If you carry out the task, use the codes in the Booklet to mark the proper answers. Then move on to the next task. MARK THAT TASK AND ALL THE REST IN PART I USING THE SAME CODES FOR (A) and (B). Keep going until you've finished Part I.

If you have any problems, please feel free to check with the monitor.

I. DIRECT CLINICAL	A	B
(1) Try to locate people who might need services or financial assistance by means of home visits, telephone calls, or talks with clients.	(65)	
(2) Go to group meetings (e.g., tenants' associations, client groups) to learn more about clients' needs and problems.	(67)	
(3) Inform clients about services and/or resource locations in order to promote utilization of resources.	(69)	
(4) Give information to clients, relatives, or other people in order to explain and interpret agency programs, policies, or procedures.	(71)	
(5) Carry out standard procedures (fill out forms, write memos, inform supervisor) in order to refer client(s) to appropriate service resources.	(73)	
(6) Take clients to specific places, (using agency or personal car) to link client with service or treatment resource.	(75)	
(7) Talk with co-workers (inside or outside of the agency) in order to help clients get a more favorable service action or to get improved services.	(77)	
(8) Discuss client needs with lay people (e.g., employer, clergy, landlord) in order to get better treatment for clients.	(79)	

-3-

[2]

	A	B
(9) Talk with clients (or relatives) about problems, answering questions when necessary, in order to reassure, support, and release anxiety.	(30)	
(10) Talk with clients about problems in order to help adjustment or promote "responsible" behavior.	(32)	
(11) Talk with clients about a specific problem, answering questions when necessary, offering advice when indicated, in order to resolve the problem.	(34)	
(12) Re-establish order (referee, advise, separate) in an argument (or fight) between clients.	(36)	
(13) Help out in a problem situation or a disagreement between client(s) and an agency worker or representative (vendor).	(38)	
(14) Discuss problems with client(s), defining needs and answering questions, in order to help select a course of action.	(40)	
(15) Teach and help client(s) in the use of writing, composition, and/or spelling.	(42)	
(16) Observe or supervise client's work (or chores), giving instruction as needed.	(44)	
(17) Teach client(s) about hygiene, personal grooming, or care of clothing.	(46)	
(18) Instruct client(s) in food preparation and housekeeping skills to help improve home-making capabilities.	(48)	

-4-

	A	B

II. INDIRECT CLINICAL

(29) Use telephone or other methods to arrange for or find transportation for client(s).] (70)]

(30) Discuss job vacancies or positions with employers to help clients find jobs.] (72)]

(31) Interview clients (in home or office) or review applications and complete paperwork, as required, in order to determine initial or continuing eligibility (for services, foodstamps, or financial assistance).] (74)]

(32) Explain service or client needs to people in order to encourage them to become resources (for example, volunteers, contractors).] (76)]

(33) Describe unmet service needs (or proposed plan) to a legislator or other officials, using telephone, letters, or personal visit, in order to get legislative or administrative support.] (78)]

[3]

(34) Explain social or service programs to lay people (in office meetings, speeches, T.V. interviews) in order to inform people of the programs.] (30)]

(35) Suggest or propose a plan to workers (or superiors) in order to gather needed support for a change in services, procedures, or rules.] (32)]

(36) Gather information about a home or other resource in order to license/approve (or help someone else to do so) the resource for use by clients.] (34)]

---

(19) Teach client(s) skills relating to money, computations, and budgeting in order to develop skills in management.] (50)]

(20) Work with clients to teach them how to behave in group situations.] (52)]

(21) Prepare and/or serve meals for client(s), either individually or from central-ized kitchen.] (54)]

(22) Change linens, clean up dishes, or carry out other housekeeping tasks for client(s).] (56)]

(23) Bathe, shave, and/or wash client(s) in order to increase personal comfort or to improve personal appearance.] (58)]

(24) Help client(s) in dressing and/or grooming themselves in order to prepare them for daily activities.] (60)]

(25) Run errands, do shopping, carry out light chores for client(s).] (62)]

(26) Give medicine to client(s) according to procedures or observe to see that medicines are being taken by client(s).] (64)]

(27) Treat or dress rashes, cuts, pressure areas, etc., or carry out other minor first aid.] (66)]

(28) Provide or participate in leisure activities (games, party, T.V., conversation) with client(s) at home or in center or other care setting.] (68)]

III. PROGRAMMING AND DIRECTING WORK (SELF)

(37) Review case schedule (reviews, visits, etc.) in order to plan your activities for a given work period.   A [ ] (36)   B [ ]

(38) Review file and records of client(s) prior to an interview, recertification, or visit in order to plan a course of action.   A [ ] (38)   B [ ]

(39) Consult a worker (usually a superior or consultant) regarding a client, exchanging information about case details, in order to get direction or advice in dealing with the case.   A [ ] (40)   B [ ]

(40) Examine and review materials (mail, administrative letters, memos) in order to set priorities and plan your work activities.   A [ ] (42)   B [ ]

(41) Interview client(s) or relative(s), using available information in order to carry out intake with the client.   A [ ] (44)   B [ ]

IV. PROGRAMMING AND DIRECTING WORK (OTHERS)

(42) Go over case record(s) of subordinate(s) in order to insure that documentation (e.g., recording, correspondence, etc.) has been carried out according to proper procedures.   A [ ] (46)   B [ ]

(43) Rate worker's (subordinate) performance, using performance rating form and dictating narrative when necessary.   A [ ] (48)   B [ ]

(44) Discuss work evaluation with worker (subordinate) in order to promote understanding of job expectations or to work out any grievances or differences.   A [ ] (50)   B [ ]

(45) Give worker(s) advice with regard to personal or job-related problem(s) in order to restore job functioning.   A [ ] (52)   B [ ]

(46) Schedule (coordinate) working hours, vacations, etc., informing employees according to procedure, in order to arrange adequate staffing patterns and coverage.   A [ ] (54)   B [ ]

(47) Review case records in order to assign (reassign) cases to unit or staff members.   A [ ] (56)   B [ ]

(48) Clarify job duties, roles, and work assignments for your workers in order to increase individual or group effectiveness.   A [ ] (58)   B [ ]

V. DEVELOPMENT (SELF)

(49) Review administrative literature (manuals, letters, memos) in order to become familiar with (or review) agency policies and procedures.   A [ ] (60)   B [ ]

(50) Take part in regularly scheduled discussions with co-workers, discussing events of the day, problems or interactions with particular clients in order to develop knowledge of program operations and individual clients.   A [ ] (62)   B [ ]

VI. DEVELOPMENT (OTHERS)

(51) Teach group of workers, in classroom or other setting, according to a training plan, in order to increase knowledge (or skills) of staff.   A [ ] (64)   B [ ]

-6-   [4]

A B

(52) Review case(s) with colleague (subordinate), clarifying and evaluating case situation, recommending methods and approaches, in order to instruct worker in dealing with case situations.   (66)

(53) Go over policies, procedures, or laws with worker(s) or subordinate(s), in order to inform or advise them about new or established policies or to clarify the nature of a particular program.   (68)

(54) Discuss job expectations and agency procedures (policy) with new workers in order to familiarize them with the situation or to plan training and orientation for them.   (70)

(55) Tutor individual workers in job-related procedures, helping with job assignments when indicated, in order to provide on-the-job training.   (72)

VII. INFORMATION PROCESSING

(56) Record or dictate client information (case narratives, forms) in order to update records, provide case status data, or document services provided.   (74)

(57) Visit or interview people of various kinds (relatives, employers) in order to verify statements made by clients.   (76)

(58) Draft, dictate and/or proofread correspondence to clients, workers, or other persons in order to answer inquiries or request specific action or information.   (78)

A B

(59) Fill out standard reporting forms or questionnaires in order to provide data for special studies or periodic reports about clients or the agency.   (30)

(60) Record or compile employee information about yourself or others (e.g., leave, compensatory time, mileage, attendance) in order to maintain records.   (32)

(61) Process payment vouchers in order to authorize/deny payment to vendors or resources.   (34)

(62) Fill out requisitions, vouchers to order supplies.   (36)

VIII. MANAGING WORK UNITS

(63) Compile lists of clients, workers, or other units that have certain characteristics.   (38)

(64) Use standard form or methods (e.g., work sampling, time study, etc.) in order to provide data for reimbursement, analysis, or other uses.   (40)

(65) Design or give out surveys (questionnaires, interviews) to specific groups (e.g., clients, employees, community people) in order to determine opinions for program planning or evaluation purposes.   (42)

(66) Compute numerical or statistical information in order to study characteristics or infer relationships about clients, employees, or facilities.   (44)

-7-

         A   B

(67) Plan a presentation (or agenda) or conduct meeting of co-workers in order to exchange information or determine specific administrative action.   ]] (46)

(68) Plan training program (or session), designing curriculum, scheduling periods or arranging for staff and facilities.   ]] (48)

(69) Write policy or procedural statements (occasionally with others) in order to develop/provide standard operating procedures.   ]] (50)

(70) Plan the details of a new or expanded service program or administrative unit (alone or with others).   ]] (52)

(71) Recruit and/or screen applicants, using knowledge of job requirements of vacant positions, in order to handle the manpower needs of your appropriate unit/department.   ]] (54)

(72) Calculate or record employee information (leave, travel, attendance, compensatory time) in order to report employee activities and summarize employees' status.   ]] (56)

(73) Pick up or transport supplies, valuables, or other property (including money, food-stamps) between your office and a designated location.   ]] (58)

(74) Sign routine paperwork (e.g., leave requests, purchase orders, travel expenditures) in order to provide authorized signature.   ]] (60)

         A   B

(75) Prepare or review budgets or financial (expenditure) statements for your unit (department) in order to determine or control financial status.   ]] (62)

(76) Inspect facility (e.g., building, grounds, vehicles, security posts, sanitation, furniture, equipment) while on regular walking tour in order to assess security, determine deficiencies, and monitor the status of the area.   ]] (64)

(77) Keep track of the distribution and use of supplies (foodstamps or any tangible goods) in order to insure an adequate supply for use.   ]] (66)

-8-

INSTRUCTIONS FOR PART II OF THE SURVEY

Read Part II all the way through before marking any percentages. Also read over the instruction section for Part II in the TASK SURVEY Booklet. Feel free to question the survey monitor if you are not sure about any of the cluster definitions or have questions about marking the SURVEY.

Part II - Section A -- Percentage of Time (Refers only to pages 8 and 9 below.)

1. Read the definitions for each of the Job Task Clusters. You may also find it helpful to look over the task statements listed in Part I for each cluster. This may give you a clearer idea of what each cluster contains.

2. Think of your job.

3. Reviewing your work activities for a typical month, divide your job into the eight clusters listed below. Using 100% of your time as the total limit, assign a percentage of your work time to each cluster. If you don't do any tasks in a given cluster, put a 00 in Column A. When you're through, go back and adjust as you think necessary.

4. Be sure to place a figure in Column A for each cluster even if it's a zero. Be sure the numbers in Column A add up to 100% or close to it.

5. When you've finished with Part II - Section A, look back over your answers and check particularly to make sure that Parts I and II agree with one another to your satisfaction.

TASK CLUSTERS (definitions)	A PERCENTAGE OF TIME SPENT
1. DIRECT CLINICAL - job activities which have to do with giving help, care, and assistance to clients directly. If you do anything like transporting clients, making referrals, teaching or "coaching" clients, giving physical care, or helping (counseling) clients or relatives, you should mark some percentage in Column A.	(68)
2. INDIRECT CLINICAL - Job activities which make it possible for people to receive services and financial assistance (usually from people other than you). If you do anything like making service arrangements (for example, transportation), developing resources (for example, getting volunteers, raising money), explaining programs to the public, determining eligibility for services or financial assistance, or advocating for outside support, you should mark some percentage in Column A.	(70)

-9-

TASK CLUSTERS (definitions)	A PERCENTAGE OF TIME SPENT
3. ORGANIZING AND DIRECTING WORK (SELF) - Job activities which involve scheduling and organizing your own work. If your job involves things like reviewing your schedule for cases or visits, developing a plan of service, or setting up your calendar for the day, you should mark some percentage in Column A.	(72)
4. ORGANIZING AND DIRECTING WORK (OTHERS) - Job activities in which you schedule, organize, or direct the work of other people. If you do anything like assigning cases to workers or carrying out in-take, scheduling work assignments, evaluating work performance or reviewing cases to insure that they've been handled properly, you should mark some percentage in Column A.	(74)
5. DEVELOPMENT (SELF) - Job activities which are associated with your growth and development as a worker. If you do anything in your job to improve your skills and knowledge (for example, reading technical materials, talking over problem areas with other workers), you should mark some per-centage in Column A.	(76)
6. DEVELOPMENT (OTHERS) - Job activities which are related to the teaching or training of other workers. If you do anything like plan or carry out training activities (formal or informal), conduct orientation sessions, or have conferences with other workers, you should mark some percentage in Column A.	(78)
7. INFORMATION PROCESSING - Job activities relating to obtaining or recording facts about clients, your activities, or the organization you work in. If your job involves anything like filling out forms and requisitions, doing narrative recording, or preparing correspondence, you should mark some percentage in Column A.	(30)
8. MANAGING WORK UNITS - Job activities which involve administering and directing units of any size. If your job involves any kind of program planning, evaluating service effectiveness, keeping track of supplies or materials, or any responsibility for a physical facility of some kind, you should mark some percentage in Column A.	(32)
TOTAL	100%

[5] ------

-10-

PART II - Section B -- How You Get Instructions

In this section, we'd like you to tell us how you generally get information about HOW your job is to be done and WHEN you are supposed to do various tasks.

People find out about how they are to do their job in different ways. Sometimes they find out because things are WRITTEN DOWN (policies, procedures, etc.). Sometimes, they ask or are told by supervisors or other workers and find out by WORD OF MOUTH. In other instances, they work it out for themselves and have to rely on their OWN JUDGMENT. Now, think of your job. Think of all the times you do things. Mark down, in percentages, how often you know how or when to do something:

Because it is in writing (policies, procedures, guidelines, regulations)	(34) %
Because someone tells you how or when to do it (supervisor, co-worker)	(36) %
Because you figure it out yourself and rely on your own judgment	(38) %

TOTAL: 100%

Part III. YOUR FEELINGS ABOUT YOUR JOB.

This final part deals with your reactions to your job and to certain characteristics of jobs in general. Section A asks you to indicate how well a number of brief statements describe your job. Sections B and C ask for general and specific reactions to various aspects of your job. Finally, in Section D, you are asked to indicate your preference for various kinds of jobs. As with the previous parts, make your marks in the SURVEY itself in the appropriate blanks. There are complete instructions in the front of each section. Coding instructions for Section D are in the SURVEY Booklet.

Please answer these questions as accurately as you can. In this part, there are no right or wrong answers -- the Department is mainly interested in your feelings about the work you do.

Thank you.

-11-

PART III - Section A.

Listed below are a number of statements which could be used to describe a job. Please indicate whether each statement is an accurate or inaccurate description of your job. Try to be as objective as you can in deciding how accurately each statement describes your job -- regardless of whether you like or dislike the job.

> Write a number in the blank beside each statement, based on the following scale:
>
> How accurate is the statement in describing your job?
>
> 1 - - - - - 2 - - - - 3 - - - 4 - - - 5 - - - 6 - - - - 7
> Very   Mostly   Slightly   Uncertain   Slightly   Mostly   Very
> Inaccurate   Inaccurate   Inaccurate   Accurate   Accurate   Accurate

1. ___ (40) The job requires me to use a number of complex or high-level skills.

2. ___ (41) The job requires a lot of cooperative work with other people.

3. ___ (42) The job is arranged so that I do not have the chance to do an entire piece of work from beginning to end.

4. ___ (43) Just doing the work required by the job provides many chances for me to figure out how well I am doing.

5. ___ (44) The job is quite simple and repetitive.

6. ___ (45) The job can be done adequately by a person working alone--without talking or checking with other people.

7. ___ (46) The supervisors and co-workers on this job almost never give me any "feedback" about how well I am doing in my work.

8. ___ (47) This job is one where a lot of people can be affected by how well the work gets done.

9. ___ (48) The job denies me any chance to use my personal initiative or judgment in carrying out the work.

10. ___ (49) Supervisors often let me know how well they think I am performing the job.

11. ___ (50) The job provides me the chance to completely finish the pieces of work I begin.

12. ___ (51) The job itself provides very few clues about whether or not I am performing well.

13. ___ (52) The job gives me considerable opportunity for independence and freedom in how I do the work.

14. ___ (53) The job itself is not very significant or important in the broader scheme of things.

-12-

PART III - Section B.

Each of the statements below is something that a person might say about his or her job. You are to indicate your own, personal feelings about your job by marking how much you agree with each of the statements.

Write a number in the blank for each statement, based on this scale:

How much do you agree with the statement?

1--------2--------3--------4--------5--------6--------7
Disagree   Disagree   Disagree   Neutral   Agree   Agree   Agree
Strongly   Slightly   Slightly   Strongly

1. ⌐⌐⌐ My opinion of myself goes up when I do this job well.
   (54)

2. ⌐⌐⌐ Generally speaking, I am very satisfied with this job.
   (55)

3. ⌐⌐⌐ I feel a great sense of personal satisfaction when I
   (56)   do this job.

4. ⌐⌐⌐ I frequently think of quitting this job.
   (57)

5. ⌐⌐⌐ I feel bad and unhappy when I discover that I have per-
   (58)   formed poorly on this job.

6. ⌐⌐⌐ I am generally satisfied with the kind of work I do in this
   (59)   job.

7. ⌐⌐⌐ My own feelings generally are not affected much one way or
   (60)   the other by how well I do on this job.

-13-

PART III - Section C.

Now please indicate how *satisfied* you are with each aspect of your job listed below. Once again, write the appropriate number in the blank beside each statement.

> How satisfied are you with this aspect of your job?
>
> 1- - - - -2- - - - - -3- - - - - -4- - - - -5- - - - - -6- - - - - -7
> Extremely   Dissatisfied   Slightly   Neutral   Slightly   Satisfied   Extremely
> Dissatisfied   Dissatisfied   Satisfied   Satisfied

1. ____ (61) The amount of job security I have.

2. ____ (62) The amount of pay and fringe benefits I receive.

3. ____ (63) The amount of personal growth and development I get in doing my job.

4. ____ (64) The people I talk to and work with on my job.

5. ____ (65) The degree of respect and fair treatment I receive from my boss.

6. ____ (66) The feeling of worthwhile accomplishment I get from doing my job.

7. ____ (67) The chance to get to know other people while on the job.

8. ____ (68) The amount of support and guidance I receive from my supervisor.

9. ____ (69) The degree to which I am fairly paid for what I contribute to this organization.

10. ____ (70) The amount of independent thought and action I can exercise in my job.

11. ____ (71) How secure things look for me in the future in this organization.

12. ____ (72) The chance to help other people while at work.

13. ____ (73) The amount of challenge in my job.

14. ____ (74) The overall quality of the supervision I receive in my work.

-14-

PART III - Section D. (Use the scale on page 7 of the Booklet.)

	JOB A	JOB B
1. (75)	A job where the pay is good.	A job where there is considerable opportunity to be creative and innovative.
2. (76)	A job where you often are required to make important decisions.	A job with many pleasant people to work with.
3. (77)	A job in which greater responsibility is given to those who do the best work.	A job in which greater responsibility is given to loyal employees who have the most seniority.
4. (78)	A job in an organization which is in financial trouble -- and might have to close down within a year.	A job in which you are not allowed to have any say whatever in how your work is scheduled, or in the procedures to be used in carrying it out.
5. (79)	A very routine job.	A job where your co-workers are not very friendly.
6. (80)	A job with a supervisor who is often very critical of you and your work in front of other people.	A job which prevents you from using a number of skills that you worked hard to develop.

[6]-----------

	JOB A	JOB B
7. (30)	A job with a supervisor who respects you and treats you fairly.	A job which provides constant opportunities for you to learn new and interesting things.
8. (31)	A job where there is a real chance you could be laid off.	A job with very little chance to do challenging work.
9. (32)	A job in which there is a real chance for you to develop new skills and advance in the organization.	A job which provides lots of vacation time and an excellent fringe benefit package.
10. (33)	A job with little freedom and independence to do your work in the way you think best.	A job where the working conditions were poor.
11. (34)	A job with very satisfying teamwork.	A job which allows you to use your skills to the fullest extent.
12. (35)	A job which offers little or no challenge.	A job which requires you to be completely isolated from co-workers.

-15-

```
Thank you for taking the time to complete the questionnaire.
We appreciate your help in carrying out this study of jobs
and work in the Department of Pensions and Security.  The
answers you have given will greatly aid the Department in
examining job classifications and characteristics through-
out the state.
```

Appendix D:
Final Version of the
Job Analysis Survey
Coding and Instruction Booklet
(Used February to April 1976)

This booklet contains information and coding
instructions to accompany the JOB ANALYSIS SURVEY.
Before completing any questions in the SURVEY,
please consult this booklet for directions. Do
not write anywhere in this booklet; it will be
used again by others.

2/76-2

On page 1 of the JOB ANALYSIS SURVEY, there are a number of questions
dealing with PERSONAL HISTORY. These questions, items 1 through 16, should
be answered by using the codes contained on the next several pages. Before
you answer the item, please be sure you understand the way the question
should be answered. If you have any problems, don't hesitate to ask the
person who is monitoring the questionnaire administration. When entering
information in any of the boxes, PLEASE PRINT.

PERSONAL INFORMATION

(1) NAME - Enter your last name beginning in the left-most space. Enter
    your middle initial in the space provided and start your first name
    immediately after your middle initial. If the spaces provided for
    either your last name or your first name are not sufficient, enter
    as much of each name as possible in the spaces provided.

Example: If your name is Allison F. Throckmorton, you would print

Last   MI First

| T | H | R | O | C | K | M | O | R | T | F | A | L | L | I | S | O | N | | |

(2) SOCIAL SECURITY NUMBER - Print your nine-digit Social Security Number
    in the spaces provided.

(3) DATE - This is today's date, (the date you are completing this survey).
    Be sure to have a number in every box. Enter the date using the
    following format:

    MM - DD - YY   Example: February 6, 1976 = | 0 | 2 | 0 | 6 | 7 | 6 |

(4) PAYROLL NUMBER - Enter your five-digit DPS payroll number.

(5) LOCATION - Using the following codes, enter the appropriate two-digit
    number which represents the county in which you work or, if you are
    not assigned to a single county, the bureau or division in which you
    are housed.

01 - Autauga	35 - Houston	75 - Commissioner's Office
02 - Baldwin	36 - Jackson	77 - Special Programs and
03 - Barbour	37 - Jefferson	Projects
04 - Bibb	38 - Lamar	78 - Food Assistance
05 - Blount	39 - Lauderdale	79 - Public Assistance
06 - Bullock	40 - Lawrence	80 - Adult Services
07 - Butler	41 - Lee	81 - Family and
08 - Calhoun	42 - Limestone	Children's Services
09 - Chambers	43 - Lowndes	82 - Emergency Welfare
10 - Cherokee	44 - Macon	84 - Internal Audit
11 - Chilton	45 - Madison	85 - Quality Control -
12 - Choctaw	46 - Marengo	Regular
13 - Clarke	47 - Marion	86 - Quality Control -
14 - Clay	48 - Marshall	Food Assistance

-2-

49 – Mobile	75 – Commissioner's Office
50 – Monroe	77 – Special Programs and Projects
51 – Montgomery	78 – Food Assistance
52 – Morgan	79 – Public Assistance
53 – Perry	80 – Adult Services
54 – Pickens	81 – Family and Children's Services
55 – Pike	82 – Emergency Welfare
56 – Randolph	84 – Internal Audit
57 – Russell	85 – Quality Control – Regular
58 – St. Clair	86 – Quality Control – Food Assistance
59 – Shelby	87 – Staff Development
60 – Sumter	88 – Administrative Services
61 – Talladega	89 – Management Information
62 – Tallapoosa	90 – Financial Management
63 – Tuscaloosa	92 – Field Service
64 – Walker	93 – Field Service – Services
65 – Washington	94 – Field Service – Administration
66 – Wilcox	96 – Legal Services
67 – Winston	97 – Public Affairs

---

(6) PROGRAM EFFORT – Using the following codes, enter the appropriate two-digit number which represents the program effort to which you are assigned.

01 – Adult Services	26 – Contract Service
02 – AFDC Services	05 – Adult Income Maintenance
03 – Child Welfare Services (CWS)	06 – AFDC Income Maintenance
04 – Combination Services	07 – Combination Income Maintenance
11 – WIN Services	25 – Child Support
12 – Day Care Services	09 – Food Assistance
13 – AFDC and CWS	20 – Staff Development
19 – Emergency Welfare Services	27 – Medical Care Division
	10 – Unassigned

(7) JOB CLASSIFICATION CODE – Enter the two-digit number which represents your job classification. Use the following codes:

05 – Human Services Aide I	61 – County Welfare Director I
06 – Human Services Aide II	62 – County Welfare Director II
07 – Human Services Aide III	63 – County Welfare Director III
22 – Food Asst. Field Agent	64 – County Welfare Director IV
23 – Food Asst. Field Supervisor	65 – County Welfare Director V
39 – Public Asst. Elig. Tech.	71 – Welfare Administrator I
48 – Case Work Reviewer	72 – Welfare Administrator II
51 – Social Worker I	74 – Welfare Supervisor I
52 – Social Worker II	75 – Welfare Supervisor II
53 – Case Work Supervisor	76 – Welfare Supervisor III
54 – Food Asst. Administrator I	77 – Program Activities Specialist
55 – Food Asst. Administrator II	

(8) AGE – Enter your age (to the nearest year) in the spaces provided.

-3-

(9) <u>RACE</u> - Using the following abbreviations, please enter your race in the space provided.

W - White   A - Asian American
N - Negro   L - Latin American
I - American Indian   O - Other

(10) <u>SEX</u> - Using the following abbreviations, enter your sex in the space provided.

M - Male   F - Female

(11) <u>EDUCATION LEVEL</u> - From the list below, enter the two-digit code which describes the highest education level you have attained.

00 - Less than 6th grade
01 - 6th but less than 12th grade
02 - High school graduate or equivalent (G.E.D.)
03 - Less than 2 years of college
04 - Two or more years of college without a degree
05 - Two or more years of college with an Associate degree (A.A.)
06 - Bachelor's degree (excluding BSW)
07 - Bachelor's of Social Work (BSW) degree
08 - One quarter of graduate work without Master's degree
09 - One semester of graduate work without Master's degree
10 - One year of graduate work without Master's degree
11 - One and one-half years of graduate work without Master's degree
12 - Two years of graduate work without Master's degree
13 - Master's degree
14 - Doctorate degree

(12) <u>YEAR GRADUATED</u> - Enter the last two digits of the year in which you attained the education level you indicated in question (11).

(13) <u>SCHOOL</u> - Using the following list, enter the two-digit code which represents the college or university you last attended.

00 - No college (university)   12 - Samford University
     attended   13 - Stillman College
01 - Alabama A & M   14 - Talladega College
02 - Alabama State   15 - Troy State
03 - Athens College   16 - Tuskegee Institute
04 - Auburn University   17 - University of Alabama (Tuscaloosa)
05 - AUM (Auburn Univ. -   18 - UAB (Univ. of Ala. - Birmingham)
     Montgomery)   19 - UAH (Univ. of Ala. - Huntsville)
06 - Birmingham Southern   20 - University of Montevallo
07 - Florence State   (Alabama College)
     (Univ. of N. Alabama)   21 - University of S. Alabama
08 - Huntingdon College
09 - Jacksonville State
10 - Livingston University
11 - Miles College

-4-

(14) UNDERGRADUATE MAJOR — Using the following list, enter the two-digit
code which best describes your undergraduate major.

00 — No college	07 — Physical Education
01 — Accounting	08 — Psychology
02 — Business Administration	09 — Recreation
03 — Child Development	10 — Social Work
04 — Education	11 — Sociology
05 — Home Economics	12 — Statistics
06 — Mathematics	13 — Other

(15) TIME (YEARS) IN PRESENT POSITION — Enter the number of years (to the
nearest year) you have held your present position. Be sure to have a
number in every space. For example, if you have worked in your present
position for 3 years and 7 months, you would enter 04 in the spaces
provided.

(16) DATE OF ORIGINAL APPOINTMENT TO THE DEPARTMENT — Enter the month and
year of your original appointment to the Department. Be sure to have
a number in every space. Please use the following format:

MM — YY   Example: February, 1969 = | 0 | 2 | 6 | 9 |

-5-

PART I — FREQUENCY OF ACTIVITY (Starts on page 2 of the SURVEY).

In this part of the SURVEY you will find a series of tasks which are grouped under the eight general clusters you worked with in PART I. For each of the 77 tasks, we are interested in finding out 2 things: (A) how often you do the task, and (B) whether or not it's a regular part of your job. To answer these two questions, we will use two sets of codes. The first, reflects how often you do a particular task. It is pictured below in the form of a scale:

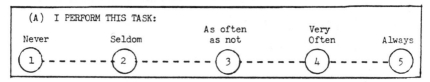

Below each statement, there is a number ranging from "1" to "5". Simply choose that statement which describes how often you do the task (in the course of a normal month) and enter that number in the box underneath the A column next to the task in question. For example, if you never carry out a particular task, you would put a "1" in Column A. If you do the task very often, you would put a "4" in the box, and so forth.

NOTE: "ALWAYS" MEANS VERY, VERY OFTEN. IT SHOULD BE USED FOR A TASK WHICH YOU DO A GREAT NUMBER OF TIMES DURING A TYPICAL WORK PERIOD.

The second question deals with whether or not the task is a regular part of your job. It can be answered simply by using the following:

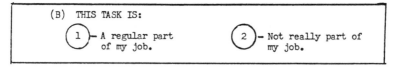

For example, if you do a particular task but, as far as you know, it's not part of your job, you would put a "2" in Column B. If it's a regular part of your job, you would put a "1" in Column B. IF YOU MARKED "1" IN COLUMN A (YOU NEVER DO THE TASK), YOU SHOULD LEAVE COLUMN B BLANK.

When you finish a given task, move on to the next one. Mark Columns A and B appropriately. Remember, if you never do a particular task, mark Column A but leave the box in Column B blank.

-6-

PART II – Section A – – PERCENTAGE OF TIME (Pages 8 and 9 of the SURVEY).

This part of the SURVEY simply asks you to divide your job time (100%) among 8 different types of tasks. You are to decide, as closely as you can, what percentage of your job time (in an average month) you spent doing each type of task. Don't worry about whether or not you <u>should</u> be doing the tasks, if you <u>actually</u> do them, please mark it down. Place your percentages in Column A.

When you put in the percentage, <u>always</u> use <u>two numbers</u> even though it's less than 10 percent.

For example, if you don't do the task <u>at all</u>: |_0 ¡ 0_|

If you spend 5 percent of your time: |_0 ¡ 5_|

If you spend 35 percent of your time: |_3 ¡ 5_|

Now read the directions on page 8 of the SURVEY and complete Section A.

PART II – Section B – – HOW YOU GET INSTRUCTIONS (Page 10 of the SURVEY).

On page 10 of the SURVEY, you will find directions for completing Section B. Basically, we are interested in how you <u>typically</u> find out about the way things are to be done on your job. You are to indicate, in terms of percentages, how often you find out about <u>when</u> and <u>how</u> tasks are to be done (a) by READING things that have been written down, (b) by WORD OF MOUTH from other people, or (c) by using YOUR OWN JUDGMENT.

Now, go ahead and read the instructions on page 10 of the SURVEY and complete **Section B.**

NOTE: REMEMBER THAT PARTS I AND II SHOULD BE CONSISTENT. IF YOU PUT A "OO" IN PART II FOR A GIVEN TASK CLUSTER (YOU SPEND NO TIME DOING THOSE TASKS), YOU SHOULD HAVE MARKED A "1" IN ALL THE TASKS FOR THAT CLUSTER IN PART I. IF THIS IS NOT THE CASE, GO BACK AND ADJUST EITHER PART I OR PART II UNTIL THEY AGREE.

———————————

PART III – YOUR FEELINGS ABOUT YOUR JOB (starts on page 10 of the SURVEY).

In this last part of the SURVEY you will find four sections (A through D) which are designed to measure your reactions to and your feelings about your job. Turn to page 10 of the SURVEY now and complete Sections A, B, and C.

———————————

PART III – Section D

People differ in the kinds of jobs they would most like to hold. The questions in this section give you a chance to say just what it is about a job that is most important to <u>you.</u>

-7-

For each question, two different kinds of jobs are
briefly described. You are to indicate which of the
jobs you personally would prefer — if you had to
make a choice between them.

In answering each question, assume that everything else about the jobs is
the same. Pay attention only to the characteristics actually listed.

$\boxed{3}$

JOB A   JOB B

A job requiring work   A job requiring work
with mechanical equip-   with other people
ment most of the day   most of the day

1- - - - - - - - 2- - - - - - 3- - - - - - - 4- - - - - - - 5
Strongly   Slightly   Neutral   Slightly   Strongly
Prefer Job A   Prefer Job A   Prefer Job B   Prefer Job B

If you like working with people and working with equipment equally
well, you would choose the "Neutral" alternative and mark the number 3 in
the box next to the job pair as has been done in the example.

Here is another example. This one asks for a harder choice — between
two jobs which both have some undesirable features.

$\boxed{2}$

JOB A   JOB B

A job requiring you to   A job located 200 miles
expose yourself to con-   from your home and family
siderable physical danger

1- - - - - - - - 2- - - - - - 3- - - - - - - 4- - - - - - - 5
Strongly   Slightly   Neutral   Slightly   Strongly
Prefer Job A   Prefer Job A   Prefer Job B   Prefer Job B

If you would slightly prefer risking physical danger to working far
from your home, you would choose alternative 2 and mark the number 2 in the
box next to the job pair as has been done in the example.

Now turn to page 14 of the SURVEY and complete Section D. For each
of the twelve items, look at each pair of jobs and mark your job preference
in the box to the left of each item by using the scale below.

| 1- - - - - - - - 2- - - - - - 3- - - - - - - 4 - - - - - - - 5 |
| Strongly Slightly Neutral Slightly Strongly |
| Prefer Job A Prefer Job A Prefer Job B Prefer Job B |

Thank you.

Appendix E:
Listing of Tasks
in Each of the
Major Practice Clusters

1. Linkage
   - (7) Talk with co-workers (inside or outside the agency) in order to help clients get a more favorable service action or improved services. (.68)
   - (8) Discuss client needs with lay people (for example, employer, clergyman, landlord) in order to get better treatment for clients. (.75)
   - (12) Reestablish order (referee, advise, separate) in an argument (or fight) between clients. (.65)
   - (13) Help out in a problem situation or a disagreement between clients and an agency worker or representative (vendor). (.62)
   - (29) Use telephone or other methods to arrange for or find transportation for clients. (.73)
   - (30) Discuss job vacancies or positions with employers to help clients find jobs. (.63)
   - (36) Gather information about a home or other resource in order to license or approve the resource for use by clients (or help someone else to do so). (.57)
2. Teaching
   - (15) Teach and help clients in the use of writing, composition, or spelling. (.71)

The number in parentheses preceding each task statement is the original item number in the Job Analysis Survey. The number in parentheses following each statement is the correlation of that item with the total cluster. It is analogous to a factor loading for the item.

(16) Observe or supervise clients' work (or chores), giving instruction as needed. (.73)

(17) Teach clients about hygiene, personal grooming, or care of clothing. (.90)

(18) Instruct clients in food preparation and housekeeping skills to help improve homemaking capabilities. (.86)

(19) Teach clients skills relating to money, computations, and budgeting in order to develop skills in management. (.86)

(20) Work with clients to teach them how to behave in group situations. (.68)

3. Counseling, Informing

(1) Try to locate people who might need services or financial assistance by means of home visits, telephone calls, or talks with clients. (.60)

(3) Inform clients about services or resource locations in order to promote utilization of resources. (.84)

(4) Give information to clients, relatives, or other people in order to explain and interpret agency programs, policies, or procedures. (.73)

(5) Carry out standard procedures (fill out forms, write memos, inform supervisor) in order to refer clients to appropriate service resources. (.80)

(9) Talk with clients (or relatives) about problems, answering questions when necessary, in order to reassure, support, and release anxiety. (.86)

(10) Talk with clients about problems in order to help adjustment or promote responsible behavior. (.84)

(11) Talk with clients about a specific problem, answering questions when necessary, offering advice when indicated, in order to resolve the problem. (.86)

(14) Discuss problems with clients, defining needs and answering questions, in order to help select a course of action. (.87)

4. Personal Care

(21) Prepare or serve meals for clients, either individually or from centralized kitchen. (.92)

(22) Change linens, clean dishes, or carry out other housekeeping tasks for clients. (.95)

(23) Bathe, shave, or wash client(s) in order to increase personal comfort or improve personal appearance. (.87)

(24) Help clients in dressing or grooming themselves in order to prepare them for daily activities. (.93)

(25) Run errands, do shopping, carry out light chores for clients. (.93)

(26) Give medicine to clients according to procedures or observe to see that medicines are being taken by clients. (.83)

(27) Treat or dress rashes, cuts, pressure areas, and so forth, or carry out other minor first aid. (.49)

(28) Provide or participate in leisure activities (games, party, TV, conversation) with clients at home or in center or other care setting. (.81)

5. Case Management (Specific)

(31) Interview clients (in home or office) or review applications and complete paperwork, as required, in order to determine initial or continuing eligibility (for services, food stamps, or financial assistance). (.79)

(37) Review case schedule (reviews, visits, and so forth) in order to plan your activities for a given work period. (.78)

(38) Review file and records of clients prior to an interview, re-certification, or visit in order to plan a course of action. (.90)

(39) Consult a worker (usually a superior or consultant) regarding a client, exchanging information about case details, in order to get direction or advice in dealing with the case. (.64)

(41) Interview clients or relatives, using available information in order to carry out intake with the client. (.84)

(56) Record or dictate client information (case narratives, forms) in order to update records, provide case status data, or document services provided. (.88)

(57) Visit or interview people of various kinds (relatives, employers) in order to verify statements made by clients. (.82)

6. Compiling Information

(63) Compile lists of clients, workers, or other units that have certain characteristics. (.78)

(64) Use standard form or methods (for example, work sampling, time study) in order to provide data for reimbursement, analysis, or other uses. (.78)

(66) Compute numerical or statistical information in order to study characteristics or infer relationships about clients, employees, or facilities. (.69)

7. External Relations

(2) Go to group meetings (for example, tenants' associations, client groups) to learn more about clients' needs and problems. (.59)

(32) Explain service or client needs to people in order to encourage them to become resources (for example, volunteers, contractors). (.75)

(33) Describe unmet service needs (or proposed plan) to legislators or other officials, using telephone calls, letters, or personal visits, in order to get legislative or administrative support. (.79)

(34) Explain social or service programs to lay people (in office meetings, in speeches, on TV, in interviews) in order to inform people of the programs. (.82)

(35) Suggest or propose a plan to workers (or superiors) in order to gather needed support for a change in services, procedures, or rules. (.72)

(65) Design or give out surveys (questionnaires, interviews) to specific groups (for example, clients, employees, community people) in order to determine opinions for program planning or evaluation purposes. (.57)

8. Management of Tangibles

(62) Fill out requisitions or vouchers to order supplies. (.73)

(73) Pick up or transport supplies, valuables, or other property (including money, food stamps) between your office and a designated location. (.76)

(76) Inspect facility (for example, building, grounds, vehicles, security posts, sanitation, furniture, equipment) while on regular walking tour in order to assess security, determine deficiencies, and monitor the status of the area. (.81)

(77) Keep track of the distribution and use of supplies (food stamps or any tangible goods) in order to ensure an adequate supply for use. (.89)

9. Program Management

(67) Plan a presentation (or agenda) or conduct meeting of co-workers in order to exchange information or determine specific administrative action. (.88)

(68) Plan training program (or session), designing curriculum, scheduling periods, or arranging for staff and facilities. (.85)

(69) Write policy or procedural statements (occasionally with others) in order to develop and provide standard operating procedures. (.78)

(70) Plan the details of a new or expanded service program or administrative unit (alone or with others). (.78)

(71) Recruit or screen applicants, using knowledge of job requirements of vacant positions, in order to handle the manpower needs of your appropriate unit or department. (.75)

(72) Calculate or record employee information (leave, travel, attendance, compensatory time) in order to report employee activities and summarize employee status. (.60)

(74) Sign routine paperwork (for example, leave requests, purchase orders, travel expenditures) in order to provide authorized signature. (.79)

(75) Prepare or review budgets of financial (expenditure) statements for your unit (department) in order to determine or control financial status. (.63)

10. Employee Supervision

(42) Go over case records of subordinates in order to ensure that documentation (for example, recording, correspondence) has been carried out according to proper procedures. (.82)

(43) Rate workers' (subordinates) performance, using performance rating form and dictating narrative when necessary. (.92)

(44) Discuss work evaluation with workers (subordinates) in order to promote understanding of job expectations or to work out any grievances or differences. (.93)

(45) Give workers advice with regard to personal or job-related problems in order to restore job functioning. (.91)

(46) Schedule (coordinate) working hours, vacations, and so forth, informing employees according to procedure, in order to arrange adequate staffing patterns and coverage. (.93)

(47) Review case records in order to assign (reassign) cases to unit or staff members. (.87)

(48) Clarify job duties, roles, and work assignments for your workers in order to increase individual or group effectiveness. (.95)

(51) Teach group of workers, in classroom or other setting, according to a training plan, in order to increase knowledge (or skills) of staff. (.86)

(52) Review cases with colleagues (subordinates), clarifying and evaluating case situations, recommending methods and approaches, in order to instruct workers in dealing with case situations. (.86)

(53) Go over policies, procedures, or laws with workers or (subordinates), in order to inform or advise them about new or established policies or to clarify the nature of a particular program. (.89)

(54) Discuss job expectations and agency procedures (policy) with new workers in order to familiarize them with the situation or to plan training and orientation for them. (.89)

(55) Tutor individual workers in job-related procedures, helping with job assignments when indicated, in order to provide on-the-job training. (.90)

11. Case Management (General)
   (40) Examine and review materials (mail, administrative letters, memos) in order to set priorities and plan your work activities. (.71)
   (49) Review administrative literature (manuals, letters, memos) in order to become familiar with (or review) agency policies and procedures. (.79)
   (50) Take part in regularly scheduled discussions with co-workers, discussing events of the day and problems or interactions with particular clients, in order to develop knowledge of program operations and individual clients. (.73)
12. Paper Flow
   (58) Draft, dictate, or proofread correspondence to clients, workers, or other persons in order to answer inquiries or request specific action or information. (.65)
   (59) Fill out standard reporting forms or questionnaires in order to provide data for special studies or periodic reports about clients or the agency. (.71)
   (60) Record or compile employee information about yourself or others (for example, leave, compensatory time, mileage, attendance) in order to maintain records. (.73)
   (61) Process payment vouchers in order to authorize or deny payment to vendors or resources. (.55)

Appendix F:
Task Attribute Rating Scale

1. CRITICALITY--How critical to the attainment of the agency mission
is the adequate performance of this task?

1 Unimportant 2 Moderately Important 3 Critical 4 Extremely
Critical

2. TIME SPAN OF DISCRETION--How long a time would elapse between
the completion or execution of the task
and the time it would ordinarily be
subject to review?

.1	2	3	4	5	6	7	8	9
0>½ day	½>1 day	.1>3 days	3>7 days	1>2 weeks	2>4 weeks	1>2 months	2>4 months	4 months up

---

Adapted from the "Requisite Task Attribute" scales of Turner
and Lawrence (1965).

3. PROBABILITY OF SERIOUS ERROR: How likely is a serious error (resulting in serious personal loss or injury to the client) in carrying out the task?

1	2	3	4	5	6	7	8	9
Negligible				Unlikely but possible				Could easily happen

4. CLARITY OF REMEDIAL ACTION--How clear is the corrective action for dealing with routine problems in the task?

1	2	3	4	5	6	7	8	9
No ambiguity at all. No need for choice and decision making. Not more than one cause for error.		Slight ambiguity. The feedback is not obvious and requires some thinking. The causes for errors are few (1-3) but no problems in deciding among them.		An error can result from a combination of several causes (3-6). Not obvious but can be worked out without too much difficulty.		An error can result from a combination of a number of causes (7 or more). Requires considerable decision making to readjust.		Very great ambiguity. The relation between causes and effect are extremely hard to identify.

Appendix G:
Mean JDS Satisfaction Scores for Matched and Mismatched Workers

Family 1[a]

GENERAL SATISFACTION

		GNS	
		Hi	Lo
MPS	Hi	6.11 (3)	6.06 (11)
	Lo	5.80 (5)	6.02 (27)

JOB SECURITY

		GNS	
		Hi	Lo
MPS	Hi	5.17 (3)	5.23 (11)
	Lo	6.10 (5)	5.46 (27)

SUPERVISION

		GNS	
		Hi	Lo
MPS	Hi	5.78 (3)	5.70 (11)
	Lo	6.47 (5)	6.28 (27)

PAY

		GNS	
		Hi	Lo
MPS	Hi	5.00 (3)	4.54 (11)
	Lo	5.40 (5)	4.98 (27)

SOCIAL

		GNS	
		Hi	Lo
MPS	Hi	6.67 (3)	6.52 (11)
	Lo	6.47 (5)	6.59 (27)

OPPORTUNITY FOR GROWTH

		GNS	
		Hi	Lo
MPS	Hi	6.33 (3)	5.57 (11)
	Lo	5.60 (5)	5.94 (27)

[a] Sample sizes are in parentheses below each mean.

Family 2[a]

GENERAL SATISFACTION

		GNS	
		Hi	Lo
MPS	Hi	5.84 (45)	5.93 (48)
	Lo	5.21 (58)	5.36 (68)

PAY

		GNS	
		Hi	Lo
MPS	Hi	4.67 (45)	5.01 (48)
	Lo	4.07 (58)	4.42 (68)

JOB SECURITY

		GNS	
		Hi	Lo
MPS	Hi	5.64 (45)	5.67 (48)
	Lo	4.96 (58)	5.39 (68)

SOCIAL

		GNS	
		Hi	Lo
MPS	Hi	5.81 (45)	5.89 (48)
	Lo	5.37 (58)	5.42 (68)

SUPERVISION

		GNS	
		Hi	Lo
MPS	Hi	5.45 (45)	5.50 (48)
	Lo	5.13 (58)	5.14 (68)

OPPORTUNITY FOR GROWTH

		GNS	
		Hi	Lo
MPS	Hi	5.37 (45)	5.54 (48)
	Lo	4.25 (58)	4.57 (68)

[a]Sample sizes are in parentheses below each mean.

Family 3[a]

GENERAL SATISFACTION

		GNS	
		Hi	Lo
MPS	Hi	5.90 (48)	5.71 (39)
	Lo	5.12 (49)	5.18 (40)

PAY

		GNS	
		Hi	Lo
MPS	Hi	4.72 (48)	4.72 (39)
	Lo	4.47 (49)	4.72 (40)

JOB SECURITY

		GNS	
		Hi	Lo
MPS	Hi	5.62 (48)	5.81 (39)
	Lo	5.01 (49)	5.57 (40)

SOCIAL

		GNS	
		Hi	Lo
MPS	Hi	6.07 (48)	5.92 (39)
	Lo	5.65 (49)	5.73 (40)

SUPERVISION

		GNS	
		Hi	Lo
MPS	Hi	5.74 (48)	5.43 (39)
	Lo	4.75 (49)	5.23 (40)

OPPORTUNITY FOR GROWTH

		GNS	
		Hi	Lo
MPS	Hi	5.77 (48)	5.62 (39)
	Lo	4.83 (49)	5.04 (40)

[a]Sample sizes are in parentheses below each mean.

Family 4[a]

GENERAL SATISFACTION

		GNS	
		Hi	Lo
MPS	Hi	6.15 (26)	5.74 (27)
	Lo	5.19 (14)	5.31 (17)

PAY

		GNS	
		Hi	Lo
MPS	Hi	5.23 (26)	4.98 (27)
	Lo	4.46 (14)	4.85 (17)

JOB SECURITY

		GNS	
		Hi	Lo
MPS	Hi	5.96 (26)	6.02 (27)
	Lo	5.64 (14)	5.59 (17)

SOCIAL

		GNS	
		Hi	Lo
MPS	Hi	5.95 (26)	5.76 (27)
	Lo	5.55 (14)	5.80 (17)

SUPERVISION

		GNS	
		Hi	Lo
MPS	Hi	5.96 (26)	5.64 (27)
	Lo	5.62 (14)	4.98 (17)

OPPORTUNITY FOR GROWTH

		GNS	
		Hi	Lo
MPS	Hi	6.14 (26)	5.63 (27)
	Lo	4.71 (14)	5.43 (17)

[a] Sample sizes are in parentheses below each mean.

Family 5[a]

GENERAL SATISFACTION

		GNS	
		Hi	Lo
MPS	Hi	5.99 (43)	6.21 (14)
	Lo	5.56 (23)	5.47 (10)

PAY

		GNS	
		Hi	Lo
MPS	Hi	4.69 (43)	5.36 (14)
	Lo	5.02 (23)	4.50 (10)

JOB SECURITY

		GNS	
		Hi	Lo
MPS	Hi	5.80 (43)	5.64 (14)
	Lo	5.65 (23)	5.65 (10)

SOCIAL

		GNS	
		Hi	Lo
MPS	Hi	6.28 (43)	6.05 (14)
	Lo	5.67 (23)	6.27 (10)

SUPERVISION

		GNS	
		Hi	Lo
MPS	Hi	5.81 (43)	5.40 (14)
	Lo	4.94 (23)	5.17 (10)

OPPORTUNITY FOR GROWTH

		GNS	
		Hi	Lo
MPS	Hi	6.07 (43)	5.96 (14)
	Lo	5.21 (23)	5.90 (10)

[a] Sample sizes are in parentheses below each mean.

Entire Sample[a]

GENERAL SATISFACTION

		GNS	
		Hi	Lo
MPS	Hi	5.97 (186)	5.88 (144)
	Lo	5.23 (157)	5.39 (174)

PAY

		GNS	
		Hi	Lo
MPS	Hi	4.79 (186)	4.94 (144)
	Lo	4.46 (157)	4.65 (174)

JOB SECURITY

		GNS	
		Hi	Lo
MPS	Hi	5.76 (186)	5.74 (144)
	Lo	5.21 (157)	5.49 (174)

SOCIAL

		GNS	
		Hi	Lo
MPS	Hi	6.00 (186)	5.94 (144)
	Lo	5.55 (157)	5.78 (174)

SUPERVISION

		GNS	
		Hi	Lo
MPS	Hi	5.72 (186)	5.52 (144)
	Lo	5.07 (157)	5.32 (174)

OPPORTUNITY FOR GROWTH

		GNS	
		Hi	Lo
MPS	Hi	5.82 (186)	5.63 (144)
	Lo	4.68 (157)	5.06 (174)

[a]Sample sizes are in parentheses below each mean.

Appendix H: Mean JDS Internal Work Motivation Scores for Matched and Mismatched Workers

Family 1

		GNS	
		Hi	Lo
MPS	Hi	6.08 (3)	6.32 (11)
	Lo	6.35 (5)	6.02 (27)

Family 3

		GNS	
		Hi	Lo
MPS	Hi	6.21 (45)	6.01 (48)
	Lo	5.43 (58)	5.76 (68)

Family 2

		GNS	
		Hi	Lo
MPS	Hi	6.11 (48)	5.94 (39)
	Lo	5.83 (49)	5.84 (40)

Family 4

		GNS	
		Hi	Lo
MPS	Hi	6.20 (26)	6.00 (27)
	Lo	6.05 (14)	5.85 (17)

Family 3

		GNS	
		Hi	Lo
MPS	Hi	6.13 (43)	6.50 (14)
	Lo	6.03 (23)	6.10 (10)

Family 5

		GNS	
		Hi	Lo
MPS	Hi	6.16 (186)	6.06 (144)
	Lo	5.72 (157)	5.84 (174)

[a] Sample sizes are in parentheses below each mean.

Bibliography

Anderson, Delwin M., and Jean M. Dockhorn. 1965. "Differential Use of Staff: An Exploration with Job-Trained Personnel." *Personal Information* 8:4–43.

Austin, Michael J. 1977. "Defining the Nature of Human Service Work for Personnel System Management." *Administration in Social Work* 1:31–41.

Baer, Betty, and Ronald Federico. 1978. *Educating the Baccalaureate Social Worker: Report of the Undergraduate Social Work Curriculum Development Project*. Cambridge, Mass.: Ballinger.

Barker, Robert L., and Thomas L. Briggs. 1968. *Differential Use of Social Work Manpower: An Analysis and Demonstration Study*. New York: National Association of Social Workers.

Barker, Robert L., and Thomas L. Briggs. 1966. "Trends in the Utilization of Social Work Personnel: An Evaluative Research of the Literature." Research Report No. 2, Utilization of Social Work Personal in Mental Hospitals Project. New York: National Association of Social Workers. Mimeographed.

Bergel, Egon E. 1962. *Social Stratification*. New York: McGraw-Hill.

Blood, Milton R., and Charles L. Hulin. 1967. "Alienation, Environmental Characteristics, and Worker Responses." *Journal of Applied Psychology* 51:284–90.

Davis, Louis E., and James C. Taylor, eds. 1972. *Design of Jobs*. Middlesex, England: Penguin Books.

Dinerman, Miriam (forthcoming). *Present Social Work Curricular Patterns: Baccalaureate and Masters*. New York: The Silberman Foundation.

Dunham, Randall B. 1977. "Reactions to Job Characteristics." *Academy of Management Journal* 20:42–65.

——. 1976. "The Measurement and Dimensionality of Job Characteristics." *Journal of Applied Psychology* 61:404–9.

Equal Employment Opportunity Commission, Civil Service Commission, U.S. Department of Labor and Department of Justice. 1980. "Adoption by Four Agencies of Uniform Guidelines on Employee Selection Procedures." *Federal Register* 43:38290–38313.

Feild, Hubert S., and Robert J. Teare. 1980. "A Conceptual Framework for Validation of Social Service Job Requirements: I—General Concepts and Background." Paper prepared for National Association of Social Workers, Washington, D.C.

Fine, Sidney A. 1967. *Guidelines for the Design of New Careers*. Kalamazoo: Upjohn Institute for Employment Research.

Fine, Sidney A., and Wretha Wiley. 1971. *An Introduction to Functional Job Analysis: A Scaling of Selected Tasks from the Social Welfare Field*. Kalamazoo: Upjohn Institute for Employment Research.

Finestone, Samuel. 1964. "Major Dimensions and Alternatives in Differential Use of Casework Staff." In "Experimentation in Differential Use of Personnel in Social Welfare." National Association of Social Workers, pp. 107–113. New York: National Association of Social Workers. Mimeographed.

Forbes, Richard. 1973. "Socialization of the Public Caseworker: Resolution of Uncertainty." Doctoral dissertation, University of Chicago.

Friedman, Georges. 1961. *The Anatomy of Work*. Glencoe: Free Press.

Galbraith, John Kenneth. 1958. *The Affluent Society*. Boston: Houghton Mifflin.

Gatewood, Robert D., and Robert J. Teare. 1976. "Paraprofessional Utilization: Motives and Job-Assignment Techniques." *The Vocational Guidance Quarterly* 25:138–45.

Gilbert, Neal, and Harry Specht. 1974. *Dimensions of Social Welfare Policy*. Englewood Cliffs, N.J.: Prentice-Hall.

Grosser, Charles R. 1969. "Using the Nonprofessional." In *Breakthrough for Disadvantaged Youth*, U.S. Department of Labor, Manpower Administration.

Hackman, J. Richard, and Edward E. Lawler. 1971. "Employee Reactions to Job Characteristics." *Journal of Applied Psychology Monograph* 55:259–86.

Hackman, J. Richard, and Mary D. Lee. 1979. *Redesigning Work: A Strategy for Change*. Scarsdale: Work in America Institute.

Hackman, J. Richard, and Greg R. Oldham. 1975. "Development of the Job Diagnostic Survey." *Journal of Applied Psychology* 60:159–70.

Hackman, J. Richard, and Greg R. Oldham. 1974a. "The Job Diagnostic Survey: An Instrument for the Diagnosis of Jobs and the Evaluation of Job Redesign Projects." Technical Report No. 4., Department of Administrative Sciences. New Haven: Yale University.

Hackman, J. Richard, and Greg R. Oldham. 1974b "Motivation Through the Design of Work: Test of a Theory." Technical Report No. 6, Department of Administrative Sciences. New Haven: Yale University.

Harrington, Michael. 1962. *The Other America: Poverty in the United States*. New York: Macmillan.

Hatchett, Paulette. 1978. "Technical Report of the Job Analysis of the Social Services Worker Positions, Vol. 2, Tables." Lansing: Department of Civil Service, Planning and Research Section.

Hoppock, Robert, 1935. *Job Satisfaction*. New York: Harper and Bros.

Jenkins, G. Douglas; David A. Nadler; Edward D. Lawler; and Cortlandt Cammann. 1975. "Standardized Observations: An Approach to Measuring the Nature of Jobs." *Journal of Applied Psychology* 60:171–81.

Katan, Yosef. 1974. "The Utilization of Indigenous Workers in Human Service Organizations." In *Human Service Organizations*, edited by Yeheskel Hasenfeld and Richard English, pp. 448-67. Ann Arbor: University of Michigan Press.

Katzell, Raymond A.; Abraham K. Korman; and Edward L. Levine. 1971. *Research Report No. 1: Overview Study of the Dynamics of Worker Job Mobility*. National Study of Social Welfare Workers, Work, and Organizational Contexts. Washington, D.C.: U.S. Department of Health, Education and Welfare, Social and Rehabilitation Service.

Kleiman, Lawrence S., and John W. Lounsbury. 1978. "Validating Procedures for Social Work Personnel." *Social Work* 23:481-85.

Korman, Abraham K.; Jeffrey H. Greenhaus; and Irwin Badin. 1977. "Personnel Attitudes and Motivation." In *Annual Review of Psychology*, edited by Mark Rosenzweig and Lyman Porter, pp. 175-96. Palo Alto: Annual Reviews.

Kroeger, Naomi. 1971. "Organizational Goals, Policies, and Output: The Dilemma of Public Aid." Doctoral dissertation, University of Chicago.

Levine, Louis. 1968. "The Antecedents of Our Currently Changing Manpower Concepts." *Poverty and Human Resources Abstracts* 3:1-13.

McCormick, Ernest J. 1976. "Job and Task Analysis." In *Handbook of Industrial and Organizational Psychology*, edited by Marvin J. Dunnette. Chicago: Rand McNally, pp. 651-96.

Mayo, Elton. 1933. *The Human Problem of an Industrial Situation*. New York: Macmillan.

National Association of Social Workers. 1980. *NASW News*. November.

Office of Career Planning and Curriculum Development for the Human Services. 1975a. *Personnel and Staff Development Planning for the Human Services*. Tallahassee: State University System of Florida. (ERIC Document Reproduction Service No. ED-119571.)

Office of Career Planning and Curriculum Development for the Human Services. 1975b. *The Florida Human Service Task Bank*. Tallahassee: State University System of Florida. (ERIC Document Reproduction Service No. ED-119572.)

Olmstead, Joseph A. 1973. *Working Papers No. 2: Organizational Structure and Climate: Implications for Agencies*. National Study of Social Welfare Workers, Work, and Organizational Contexts. Washington, D.C.: U.S. Department of Health, Education and Welfare, Social and Rehabilitation Service.

O'Toole, James, ed. 1973. *Work in America: Report of a Special Task Force to the Secretary of Health, Education, and Welfare*. Cambridge, Mass.: MIT Press.

Pearl, Arthur. 1965. *The New Careers for the Poor*. New York: The Free Press.

Pines, Ayala, and Ditsa Kafrey. 1978. "Occupational Tedium in the Social Services." *Social Work* 23:499-507.

Pines, Ayala, and Christina Maslach. 1978. "Burn-out in Mental Health Professions." *Hospital and Community Psychiatry* 4:233-37.

Reiff, Robert, and Frank Riessman. 1964. *The Indigenous Nonprofessional: A Strategy of Change in Community Action and Community Mental Health Programs*. New York: National Institute of Labor Education.

Richan, Willard C. 1961. "A Theoretical Scheme for Determining Roles of Professional and Nonprofessional Personnel." *Social Work* 6:22-28.

Richan, Willard C., and Allan R. Mendelsohn. 1973. *Social Work: The Unloved Profession.* New York: New Viewpoints.

Riessman, Frank. 1965. "The 'Helper' Therapy Principle." *Social Work* 10:27–32.

Roach, Jack L., and Orville R. Gursalin. 1967. "An Evaluation of the Concept of 'Culture of Poverty'." *Social Forces* 45:383–92.

Roethslisberger, Fritz J., and William J. Dickson. 1939. *Management and the Worker.* Cambridge, Mass.: Harvard University Press.

Rosen, Bernard C. 1959. "Race, Ethnicity and the Achievement Syndrome." *American Sociological Review* 24:47–61.

Schlesinger, Arthur M. 1965. *A Thousand Days.* Boston: Houghton Mifflin.

Schriessheim, Chester, and Jan Schriessheim. 1974. "Development and Empirical Investigation of New Response Categories to Increse the Validity of Multiple Response Alternative Questionnaires." *Educational and Psychological Measurement* 34:877–84.

Sheppard, Harold L., and Neal Q. Herrick. 1972. *Where Have All the Robots Gone?* New York: Free Press.

Sims, Henry P.; Andrew D. Szilagyi; and Robert T. Keller. 1976. "The Measurement of Job Characteristics." *Academy of Management Journal* 19:195–211.

Street, David; George T. Martin, Jr.; and Laura Kramer Gordon. 1979. *The Welfare Industry.* Beverly Hills: Sage Publications.

Suttles, Gerald D. 1979. Foreword to *The Welfare Industry*, by David Street, George T. Martin, Jr., and Laura Kramer Gordon. Beverly Hills: Sage Publications.

Taylor, Frederick. 1911. *Principles and Methods of Scientific Management.* New York: Harper and Bros.

Teare, Robert J. 1978. "Paraprofessional Utilization Issues." In *Professionals and Paraprofessionals*, edited by Michael Austin, pp. 59–74. New York: Human Sciences Press.

Teare, Robert J., and Hubert S. Feild. 1980. "A Conceptual Framework for Validation of Social Service Job Requirements: II—Preliminary Strategies." Paper prepared for National Association of Social Workers, Washington D.C.

Teare, Robert J., and Harold L. McPheeters. 1970. *Manpower Utilization in Social Welfare.* Atlanta: Southern Regional Education Board.

Thomas, Edwin J. 1978. "Generating Innovation in Social Work: The Paradigm of Developmental Research." *Journal of Social Service Research* 2:95–115.

Toren, Nina. 1969. "Semi-professionalism and Social Work: A Theoretical Perspective." In *The Semi-professions and Their Organization*, edited by Amitai Etzioni, pp. 141–95. New York: Free Press.

Turner, Arthur N., and Paul R. Lawrence. 1965. *Industrial Jobs and the Worker.* Boston: Harvard University, Graduate School of Business Administration.

U.S. Civil Service Commission. 1975. *Job Analysis: Developing and Documenting Jobs.* Washington, D.C.: U.S. Civil Service Commission, Bureau of Intergovernmental Personnel Programs, November.

U.S. Department of Health, Education and Welfare. 1974. *Research Report No. 3: Overview Study of Employment of Paraprofessionals.* National Study of Social Welfare and Rehabilitation Workers, Work, and Organizational Contexts. Social and Rehabilitation Service, April.

U.S. Department of Health, Education and Welfare. 1971. *Working Papers No. 1:*

The National Study of Social Welfare and Rehabilitation Workers, Work, and Organizational Contexts. Social and Rehabilitation Service, November.

U.S. Department of Health, Education and Welfare. 1965. *Closing the Gap.* Report of the Departmental Task Force on Social Work Education and Manpower. November.

Van Maanen, John; R. Katz; and R. Gregg. 1974. *Job Satisfaction in the Public Sector.* Report Prepared for the Economic Development Administration by the National Training and Development Service, Washington, D.C.

Ward, Joe H., and Marion E. Hook, 1963. "Application of an Hierarchical Grouping Procedure to a Problem of Grouping Profiles." *Educational and Psychological Measurement* 23:69-81.

Wilensky, Harold L. 1964. "The Professionalization of Everyone." *American Journal of Sociology* 70:137-58.

Yarmolinsky, Adam. 1968. "The Service Society." *Daedalus* 97:1263-76.

Index

Index

administrators: importance rating of, 57; as JAS job family, 52; JAS profile for, 47; JDS core job dimensions for, 82; knowledge and skills required for, 63

Alabama Department of Pensions and Security (DPS), role in present study, 22-23

Anderson, Delwin M., 8, 164

Area Redevelopment Act (ARA), rationale behind, 3

Austin, Michael, 20, 164

autonomy, relationship with job discretion, 126. *See also* Job Diagnostic Survey

Badin, Irwin, 71, 166

Baer, Betty, 35, 164

Barker, Barbara, 65

Barker, Harry, 65

Barker, Robert L., 8, 17, 164

Bergel, Egon E., 3, 164

Blood, Milton R., 70, 164

Briggs, Thomas L., 8, 17, 164

bureaucracy, implications for practice, 98-100

burnout. *See* job satisfaction; Pines, Ayala; Kafrey, Ditsa

Cammann, Cortlandt, 165

core job dimensions. *See* Job Diagnostic Survey

credentials, relevance of, 102-3

Davis, Louis E., 67, 104, 164

demographic characteristics of sample: and growth-need strength, 93-94; and internal work motivation, 95; and job satisfaction, 95; in main DPS study, 29-31; in pilot study, 24

developmental method, as method of job construction, 10

Dickson, William J., 68, 167

Dinerman, Miriam, 102, 103, 164

Dockhorn, Jean M., 8, 164

domains of living, as part of SREB model, 12-13

Dunham, Randall B., 79, 164

Economic Opportunity Act (EOA): and client involvement, 6, 8; philosophy behind, 4

eligibility workers: importance rating of, 57; as JAS job family, 49-50; JAS profile for, 46; JDS core job dimensions for, 82; knowledge and skills required for, 63

episode of service, as basis for work assignment, 8

Equal Employment Opportunity Commission, 103, 164

About the Author

Robert J. Teare is Director of Research and Professor of Social Work at the University of Alabama. Until 1976, he was an Associate Professor of Management at the University of Georgia.

Dr. Teare has been a manpower consultant to social service, mental health, and educational organizations throughout the country. He has published widely. His monograph *Manpower Utilization in Social Welfare*, coauthored with Harold McPheeters, has become a classic in the field and is used as a model for many undergraduate social work programs.

Dr. Teare received the B.S. from St. Louis University and the M.S. and Ph.D. from Purdue University.